Where Are They Now?
Life After Leeds United

Summer
2005

Published by YFP

Written by
Les Rowley and John Wray
with additional material by Robert Endeacott.

Editorial Assistants
Jo Johns and Camille Jackson.

All photographs by Andrew Varley.

Printed by Clifford Press.

Thanks to all the former Leeds United players who
gave up their time and to all the people who put us in
contact with them. You know who you are.

Also thanks to **Peter Lorimer and the Leeds United
book forum group - Peter, Eddie, Giles, Geoff and
Gary.**

Former Players

Micky Adams
Mark Aizlewood
Jack Ashurst
Neil Aspin
Ian Baird
Steve Balcombe
Peter Barnes
Mick Bates
David Batty
Mark Beeney
Paul Beesley
Jim Beglin
Rod Belfitt
Noel Blake
Billy Bremner
Tomas Brolin
Tony Brown
John Buckley
Kenny Burns
Aidan Butterworth
Eric Cantona
Brian Caswell
Jeff Chandler
Lee Chapman
Jack Charlton
Trevor Cherry
Allan Clarke
Terry Connor
Terry Cooper
Andy Couzens
Tony Currie

Alan Curtis
Bobby Davison
Mervyn Day
Ken De Mange
Martin Dickinson
John Donnelly
Tony Dorigo
Keith Edwards
Roger Eli
Roy Ellam
Wayne Entwhistle
Chris Fairclough
Neil Firm
Brian Flynn
Johnny Giles
Arthur Graham
Eddie Gray
Frank Gray
Brian Greenhoff
Peter Haddock
Gunnar Halle
Peter Hampton
Gary Hamson
Ray Hankin
Carl Harris
Paul Hart
David Harvey
John Hawley
John Hendrie
Vince Hilaire
Kevin Hird

Steve Hodge
Norman Hunter
Denis Irwin
Richard Jobson
Matthew Jones
Mick Jones
Vinnie Jones
Joe Jordan
Chris Kamara
Dylan Kerr
David Kerslake
Glan Letheran
Andy Linighan
Peter Lorimer
John Lukic
Paul Madeley
Phil Masinga
Gary McAllister
John McClelland
George McCluskey
Bobby McDonald
Billy McGhie
John McGoldrick
John McGovern
Duncan McKenzie
David McNiven
Gordon McQueen
Jon Newsome
John O'Hare

David O'Leary
Brendan Ormsby
Carlton Palmer
Keith Parkinson
Derek Parlane
John Pearson
John Pemberton
Terry Phelan
Paul Reaney
David Rennie
Andy Ritchie
David Robertson
David Rocastle
Ian Rush
Alex Sabella
Scott Sellars
Lee Sharpe
John Sheridan
Carl Shutt
Lyndon Simmonds
Ronnie Sinclair
Glynn Snodin
Ian Snodin
Gary Sprake
Mel Sterland
Byron Stevenson
David Stewart
John Stiles
Gordon Strachan
Frank Strandli
Peter Swan
Bob Taylor
Gwyn Thomas
Mickey Thomas
Imre Viradi
Ray Wallace
Rod Wallace

Andy Watson
David White
Chris Whyte
David Whyte
Andy Williams
Gary Williams
Frank Worthington
Nigel Worthington
Tommy Wright
Tony Yeboah
Terry Yorath

Current Fans
(without whose support this book would not have seen the light of day)

Frank Aagaard
John Adlard
Bunmi Aina
Robert Atkinson (York)
Tracey Bagnall
Terry Barker
Paul Bates
Steve Batty
G Beckett
Andy Bell
Mike Bellwood
David Boddy
John L Borg
Phil Bowden
Bernard Boylan
Nigel Boynton
Davy Brownlee
Buddy & Snips
D Bushell
Graham Byrne
S Caddey
Bruce Carlton
Billy Carter
Nic Caruso
Tim Carvell
Les Cawdron
Jessica Cawdron
Nigel P Chambers
Anthony Chappell
Colin Coleman
Peter Collinson
David J Cook

Niall Courtney
Roy Cross
Denis Curran
Andrew Davidson
Paul Davies
Ian & Sandi Daykin
Chris Deighton
Malcolm Eastwood
Ralph Ellis
Paul Fenton
Andrea Finch
Jim Forbes
David Fowler
Neil Gardner
Zo J Gladden
Richard Gledhill
Michael Green
Steen Hansen
Paul Harrison
Steve Hasnip
Hallgeir Hellan
Ron Holgate
Lorraine Janiczek
Pat Kelly
Melvin Kelman
David Kelman
Stewart Kemble
John Kennedy
Gary Kinney
Daniel Lambert
Ted Linehan
Dr Carl Littlewood

David Maidment
June Maltpress
Joseph Markley
Terry Mosley
Martin Mulford
Kevin W Mulligan
D Nicholls
Kelvin Nicholls
Ola Nylend
Stephen O'Brien
Andrew Oddy & Julie Hirst
Frank O'Regan
Ken Piercy
Robin Priestley
Paul Punter
Robert Purcell
John Purcell
Billy Rae
Steven Ross
Dominic Rowan
Mark Rowley
Mark Ryan
Richard Share
Andrew Simmonds
Patrick Smith
Martyn Smith
Peter Stanford
R Stead
Neil Stephenson
Philip Sunter
Chris Tams
Aaron Lee Taylor
Simon Thompson

Simon J
Titchmarsh
David Tremlett
Bill Tunnicliffe
Jack Varley
Pete Vickers
Kjell Bjorn Vinje
William Wang
Dave Waring
(Now In
Australia)
David Welch
Daphne While
Rob Whitehead
& Family (York
Whites)
Tony Whiteley
Mick & Gillian
Wild
Tony Williams
(Gosport)
Archie Williams
(Gosport)
Todd Wilson
K Wilson
Christopher
Winn
Jonathan A
Woodhead
Christopher R
Woodhead
www.bobdun-
ning.net
Jonathan Wynne
Carl Yeoman

Introduction

The stage life of a footballer comes in two acts. The first is full of excitement and drama and the second holds all the tragedy and despair. No matter how good you were as a player, you get old and that's life. It's God's way of telling you to pack it in or play on at Bradford City.

One day you're a promising 18 year-old making your debut and the next, over the hill crippled by injury, with no pace and failing mental agility: outcome – you're traded in for a younger model. And how many players prepare for that cuckoo clock day when biology comes calling?

This book came out of a conversation I had with Allan Clarke in 2000. After all he did for Leeds United he was left selling industrial fume extractors and welding kits. No mention of swimming pools, Rolls Royces or the Riviera (only the Revie Era). So if that's Allan Clarke's story, what happened to the lesser lights that lit our famous footballing stage? **Where Are They Now?** was born.

The criterion for this book is simple. You must have retired from playing football (sorry David Wetherall) and have played for Leeds United from 1970. Why 1970? Well that's when football got interesting. Also there are no 'on loan' players here (sorry Neil McNab) or players who came on only as substitute (sorry Tony Arins). The words come from interviews we did with the ex-players themselves.

Some players did however slip the net. This isn't through lack of trying. We can only assume they are living with Lord Lucan. We do hope they resurface when we plan to update this book.

Les Rowley 2005.

A few words from Peter Lorimer...

When I was approached to get involved in a book about former Leeds United players I was instantly interested. Why wouldn't I be? I played over 700 games for the club and still live in the City. I see a few of the old boys like Allan Clarke and Mick Jones but mostly I have no idea what the ex-players are doing. For me this was like footballersreunited.

I went into the pub trade but am lucky to be still involved at Elland Road. I say lucky because at whatever level you played or however good you were, the game never owed you a living once you hung up the boots. All the guys in the book will tell you that.

We all had to find another way of earning money to pay the bills. One minute you are running out in front of a packed house and the next contemplating life as a Big Issue seller. Not that drastic, football isn't the most transferable or academic of careers and it was all we knew. That's one reason why I am pleased to see most of the lads finding other enjoyable and fruitful careers long after their playing days have ended.

Enjoy the book and good luck to all those players.

Peter Lorimer.

Micky Adams

Age: 43.
Alternative career to football management: Hollywood stunt double for Michael J Fox.
Games: 89 (3 goals).
Position: Attacking left-back.
Era: Late 1980s.
Leeds high point: Scoring in the 1987 FA Cup quarter final against Wigan.
After Leeds: Southampton, Stoke and Fulham.
Retired: 1996.
Then what? Became manager of Fulham in 1996 who were 91st in the League. He earned promotion in his first season but

was sacked when Mohammed Al Fayed put his millions into the club and gave Ray Wilkins the job. Dummy.
Harrods' loss: Micky went on to manage Swansea but left after just 11 days. Next it was Brentford in 1998 and then Nottingham Forest in 1999 as assistant to Dave Bassett.
Followed by: In 2000 Adams won the Division 3 title with Brighton. In 2001, with Brighton riding high in Division 2, Adams left to join his old mate Dave Bassett who had moved on to Leicester.
The big time at last? Although they were in the Premier League at the time, Leicester were facing relegation. Still, he was only the assistant to the manager.
Didn't Gary Lineker save them from administration? Yes, with a little help from a bag of crisps. Subsequently Bassett was moved 'upstairs' and Adams took over as manager and got them back into the Premiership...and then down again.
But they'll be back: Not with Adams. Following a poor start to the 2004/05 season he was booted out.
Managerial style: Long ball, route one.
Least likely to say: *'I'm organising a club trip to La Manga'.*
Potential: A future Leeds manager. He's linked with every job going so it isn't surprising he was named as the new Coventry boss in January 2005. They finished the Championship season just 2 points away from being relegated so he has a lot of work on his hands.

Mark Aizlewood

Age: 46.
Position: Midfield & captain.
Appearance: A dodgy plastic surgeon.
Era: Bremner/Wilkinson.
Strengths: Tackling, passing, heading and kicking.
Weakness: Speed, skill, and discipline.
Best game: *"The fans would say I did not have one."*
Languages: Welsh & Adidas - he let his boots do the talking.
International career: 39 caps for Wales (9 gained at Leeds).
Manager would say: "*Solid*".
The end is nigh: He gave the

Kop the 'V' sign and was stripped of the captaincy and promptly shipped off to Bradford City.
After that: He moved on to Bristol City in 1990 then to Cardiff City, his spiritual home. Non-league Aberystwyth beckoned in 1996 and he then became player/coach at Carmarthen Town in 1997. Finally, on to Cwmbran Town as assistant manager in 2003.
A Moses among men? He became the Welsh FA's version of Howard Wilkinson preaching the game of Welsh football to the young Valley dwellers. Very successful too.
Giving something back to the game: You don't get to the position of Welsh Under-17 Manager without knowing your seaweed from your larvae bread.
A future Wales manager? Tricky one. In 2002 he assaulted a BBC TV presenter and ended up in court.
Doh! As a result he lost his job as Technical Director with the FA in 2004 and not surprisingly his Welsh commentator's role.
On the plus side: He is a qualified coach with more badges than an ambitious boy scout. He's in demand.
Where? Chester for one. He went there as Ian Rush's number 2 in 2004 but was sacked in April 2005.
Currently lives: At home and assessing the job offers.
If he wasn't in football: *"I'd be very rich"*. He has non-footballing NVQ type business interests outside the game in America but would not expand.

Jack Ashurst

Age: 51.
Point of entry: Coatbridge, Scotland.
Games: 106 (1 goal - against Derby in 1987).
Era: 1986-1989.
Arrived from: Carlisle for just £35,000. A Bremner bargain buy, even though he was 31 when he joined.
Position: Centre-half and occasional captain.
Role: Stopper and nothing fancy.
Little known fact: Jack was with Sunderland in 1973, although did not play in the Cup

Final. He followed manager Bob Stokoe to Blackpool then Carlisle.
After Leeds: Doncaster Rovers from 1988 (managed by Bremner).
Retired: 1992. Jack did play a season for non-league Frickley Athletic thereafter, but finally hung his boots up after breaking his ankle in a charity match.
So where was home after football? The Northeast. He moved back to Sunderland to run his own electrical goods shop.
Electricity? In Sunderland? Some of the posh folk even have colour television and Betamax video recorders. Despite his 7-year stint with Sunderland and his fame as an ex-pro, Jack sold up after 5 years when business wasn't doing so well.
You mean he pulled the plug on it? What's he doing nowadays? He lives in Wetherby and works for Golden Fry Food Ltd in their warehouse. Jack packs dry vegetable products for transport to the big supermarkets – gravy granules are a speciality of the house.
Hobbies: The usual stuff. He likes playing golf, and watching football.
Leeds high points: The near victorious 1986-87 season of the FA Cup & play-off adventures. Not surprisingly, they were also the low points.
Favourite band: Queen.
Off-spring: Jack's son Warren is a freelance sports journalist and works in Leeds.

Neil Aspin

Age: 40 going on 41.
Era: 1982-1989.
Debut: Against Ipswich as a 16-year-old, in 1982.
Games: 241 (6 goals).
Position: Full-back.
Accolades: Neil was the supporters' Player of the Year in 1985.

Least likely to say: *"Do you think I'd leave a club like Leeds for Port Vale?".* Soon after Mel Sterland's arrival he was sold to Port Vale for £200,000.
Did he serve them well? He was treated like a star during his ten seasons at the club. Even Robbie Williams turned up to play in his testimonial in 1999.
Other clubs: Darlington and Hartlepool.
Retired: 2001 – although he did play non-league for the Conference North team Harrogate Town until 2004, where he was also assistant coach.
What made Neil leave Harrogate? His contract was not renewed which didn't go down too well in the Aspin household. He picked up some work scouting for York City and also applied for a couple of management jobs in the lower divisions as he had all the credentials. It was only a matter of time before he re-entered the game.
Where did he eventually turn up? His old stomping ground in Harrogate. It was former Leeds United chairman Bill Fotherby who asked Neil to go back to Harrogate Town as manager.
Any other Leeds connections at the club? David Batty is currently the vice president.
So going back to his Leeds United days what will Aspin be remembered for? He was so determined to play in the FA Cup semi-final 1987, that he postponed his wedding.
Forgiven? That decision to rearrange the big day caused a problem or two at the time, but Diane forgave him and realised just how much it meant to Neil to play in an FA Cup semi-final.
Family life: Neil and Diane live in Wakefield with two kids.

Ian Baird

Age: 41.
Born: 1st April.
Leeds era: 2 spells. 1985-1987 and 1988-1990.
Games: 190 (goals 58).
Other clubs: Southampton, Cardiff (loan), Newcastle (loan), Portsmouth, Middlesbrough, Hearts, Bristol City, Plymouth, and Brighton.
Retired: 1998 due to injury.
'Bairdy' the manager: 'Bairdy' has been manager of Havant and Waterlooville in the Conference South since Christmas, 2004. When we spoke they had just taken 10

points out of 12 but were struggling and by the end of the 2005 season they had finished mid-table.

Where did Ian get the management bug? In Hong Kong. He was there for 3 years before he took charge of a first division side and coached the Hong Kong national side for the Asian Cup qualifiers in 1999.

Any language problems? The culture was completely different, but Ian had an interpreter/coach.

What about discipline? 'Bairdy' was often in trouble during his playing career but as a manager he expects his troops to play with controlled aggression and avoid being stupid.

So has it worked? Well, H&W do have a problem but Ian's working on it!

Is playing or managing more rewarding? There's no substitute for playing. You can do all the preparation in the world but you can't influence much once the players cross that white line.

Other jobs? Ian worked for a Leeds-based football agent for three years after returning from Hong Kong, but didn't really enjoy it. H&W train on Tuesday and Thursday nights and play on Saturdays, so Ian has time to run a contract hire and vehicle leasing company called IBMH (stands for Ian Baird Motor Holdings) which he started up two years ago. If you need a vehicle try his website www.ibmh.co.uk.

Lives: Southampton with his second wife and two teenage children.

Steve Balcombe

Age: 43.
Position: Centre-forward.
Games: 2 (1 goal).
Era: 1981.
Leeds high point: Scoring on his debut against Aston Villa.
After Leeds: Home Farm, Dundalk, Shamrock Rovers and Oaklands (all Irish clubs).
Retired: 1985. Steve returned to England to play part-time with Whitby Town, managed by David Harvey. To supplement his meagre earnings Steve decided to try his hand at running a pub rather than spending his money in one.

Time gentlemen please: He ran *The Three Cups* in Stamford Bridge from 1985-87, *The Duke of Wellington* in East Keswick from 1987-91, *The Bull* in West Tanfield for a short while and then *The Crown* in Great Ouseburn to 2000.
So his football sort of went down the drain? He played for Harrogate Town and later for Collingham and Tadcaster but his beer-belly was getting rather noticeable.
Fully retired from all sport (except darts): 2002, but that's a bit unfair since Steve did a triathlon in 2003.
Nowadays: He's the proprietor of *The Victoria* (formerly *The Huntsman*) in Cattal, North Yorkshire, where the food and ale are reportedly top notch.
Little known fact: As a teenager in Dublin, Steve was learning to play guitar and a drumming pal invited him to an audition. Steve wasn't exactly a great guitarist and didn't get the gig.
That's not very interesting: Well, the drummer was Larry Mullen and the band would become U2. Doh!
Steve clearly lacked the 'edge'. Has he still not found what he's looking for? He's doing very well thank you and enjoying it, though it's hard work.
Ambitions: To be the Wayne Rooney of the pub trade and to bring down his golf handicap. He is married to Gillian with two sons: William aged 3 and Thomas aged 1. Steve would love them to become professional footballers.
Most likely to say: *"Never trust a landlord who doesn't sup his own beer."*

Peter Barnes

Age: 48.
Appearance: Hairdresser.
Games: 64 (6 goals).
Era: 1981-82 & 1983-84
Weakness: Defending.
Tactics: He dribbled past as many players as he could, ran to the dead ball line and crossed for someone to nod in.
Leeds highlight (personally): Signing for £930k. Kerrching!
If that wasn't enough: He also got a wedge out of putting his name to those elastic training balls in the 1980s.
Low point: Relegation in 1982.
Other clubs: Man City, WBA,

Real Betis, Coventry, Man United, Hull, Bolton, Port Vale, Farense, Sunderland, Melbourne City, and Tampa.
Amazing fact: He was one of the few Leeds flops that never went to play for Bradford City.
Retired: 1992. He then managed Runcorn briefly but could not operate with the thriftiness of lower league football. He dabbled in insurance (Peter cannot remember their name) and then got the media bug with slots on Manchester local radio.
And on to greener pastures: In 2000 Peter joined Recomac Ltd. They have a division called Kik Off Ltd and he is a Sales Director selling 3rd generation artificial turf. It's mainly used for indoor 5-a-side and outdoor hockey pitches.
Who are his customers? The Sports Council and people like us who want better facilities to play sport on. He loves it.
What about the media stuff? He has a regular column for Manchester online (generally telling Stuart Pearce he needs to pick 11 wingers each week), and predictably he does match day corporate entertaining with Manchester City.
Hobbies: Golf, keeping fit, likes a bit of soul music. He also runs the Man City veterans 5-a-side team.
Does he have any of the money left from his signing on at Leeds? It went towards buying a new house which he sold when he left the club for the second time.

Mick Bates

Age: 58.
Position: Midfield.
Appearance: Suave, sophisti-
cated importer of Turkish
Delight.
Role: A stopgap when Bremner
and Giles weren't available.

A waste of talent? He could
have walked into any other side.
Southampton came in with a
£100,000 bid, which was a lot in
those days, but because it was a
joy to be at Elland Road he
decided to stay.
Leeds era: 1964-1976.
Games: 171 (9 goals).
High point: Scoring an away
goal that secured the UEFA Cup for the club in 1968.
Other clubs: Walsall, Bradford City (mandatory for over the hill
Leeds players), Doncaster Rovers, Bentley Victoria.
Retired: 1981.
Did he have any insurance? No, but he soon did have when
he set up a successful insurance business of his own.
Who was his first client? Billy Bremner. Mick had built up a
reputation among his ex team-mates for being trustworthy so
many of them put their insurance in his hands.
Did he have the gift of the gab? He wasn't a natural salesman, but you have to make a living. He was in the business for
21 years and at the age of 52 he decided to retire.
When was that? In 1999.
Did he become bored after retiring so young? He wasn't
qualified to do anything else and being self-employed meant he
was never a nine-to-five man. He manages to fill his days.
Doing what? Mick plays a lot of golf. His first sporting love,
apart from football, was tennis but knee problems from his
footballing days meant he had to pack his racket away.
Where does he play golf? Mainly at his local course just
outside Bawtry and at Pannal, near Harrogate, with Eddie Gray
and Peter Lorimer.
How proud is he of playing in the great Revie team? He's
proud that he was considered good enough to hold his own with
that world class Leeds team.

David Batty

Age: 36
Leeds era: 1985-1993, and 1998-2004.
Games: 360 (4 goals).
Other clubs: Blackburn, and Newcastle.
Position: Midfield.
Retired: 2004.
Family man: *"My life isn't complicated at all. Most of my spare time is spent at home with my family. I enjoy them more than anything else in my leisure time."*
Other interests: Motorcycle racing. He owns a Ducati and is a big fan of Carl Fogarty. Batts

once rode the Castle Donnington circuit on a 500cc Yamaha prior to the British Grand Prix in 1999. David O'Leary would not have been happy.
Life's one big holiday: He always preferred taking Mandy and the two 11 year old boys, Jack and George, to holiday camps rather than plush hotels because he wanted them to grow up in as normal an environment as possible.
Will he be tempted to become a football manager? *"I can rule out any possibility of being tempted to try management. Management and all the hassle that goes with it has no appeal for me whatsoever."* He also hated training as a player so couldn't possibly contemplate it as a coach.
The treatment table: Injuries marred his second spell at Elland Road and when David broke a rib in his first match back he needed pain-killers for a heart problem brought on by the injury. He once aggravated the Achilles injury when it was run over by his toddler on a tricycle.
That penalty miss: David is remembered by many for his penalty miss against Argentina, when England crashed out of the World Cup. He is also remembered for the very few goals he scored – all of them spectacular.
On the board: David is vice-president of Harrogate Town FC so you will catch him there on evenings when there are club matters to discuss.
Lives: Boston Spa.

Mark Beeney

Age: 38.
Position: Goalkeeper.
Seasons: 7.
Before Leeds: Gillingham, Maidstone, Aldershot and Brighton.
Nickname: Beano.
Reason for retirement: Achilles injury, ruptured in reserve game against Stoke in 1999.
High point: Beating Man Utd on Boxing Day and playing nearly a whole season in 1993/94.
After Leeds: Brief spell at Doncaster Rovers as cover between the sticks. Never got a game so he was perfectly suited to the role.

What does an injured, reserve keeper do after quitting? He sets up an executive car chauffeur business called 'Platinum Premier Cars'. Initially based in Leeds, the company won the Sky contract through his old mate Chris Kamara and was responsible for chauffeuring Sky presenters around the country.
What did that involve? Was he sitting around, waiting for work? Bit like what he did at Leeds? Beeney was a loyal servant at Leeds I will have you know. If it wasn't for John Lukic or Nigel Martyn or Paul Robinson he might have become England's number 1. The fact he was a great keeper was the reason Leeds kept him for so long.
Glad we've straightened that one out: In 2000 he moved back down to Kent to take a part-time job with Chelsea as their Under-21 goalkeeping coach.
Football's in his blood: Indeed it is and in 2002 he was also managing Sittingbourne FC (The Brickies) part-time as well as running the car business.
Have we a happy ending? Mark went back to Chelsea full-time as reserve goal-keeping coach in 2004. He is part of the Abramovich revolution but denies he's on £50,000 a week.
Was he tapped up for the job? If he was, now is the time for Sittingbourne to sue.
Most likely to say: *"You play, I'll keep your seat warm."*
If he hadn't been a goalkeeper: Car mechanic.

Paul Beesley

Born: Liverpool.
Age: 40.
Leeds era: 1995-1997.
Games: 37 (0 goals).
Position: Defence.
Other clubs: Too many to mention. He came from Sheffield United for £250,000 and was one of Howard Wilkinson's swan song signings. If ever there was evidence needed that the manager was going off the rails then here it was.

Retired: 2001 at Chester City.
The guy's on fire: Paul and his family had a lucky escape in March 2005, when an electrical fault caused their four-bedroom home in Dronfield to catch fire. He helped his wife and three children, aged five, seven and eight, to safety just before the roof collapsed and burning debris fell into their bedrooms.
Today: Paul coaches Nottingham Forest's Under-14s and is doing a cracking job. He went to Forest after leaving Stockport County where he worked under Carlton Palmer. We phoned his previous employer and confirmed that he had his foot in the door at Stockport as kit man.
Lives: Although a Merseysider, he later settled in the Sheffield area and was Sheffield United's Player of the Year in 1993.
FA Cup friend or foe: Paul played against Leeds United for Wigan in the FA Cup quarter-final at Springfield Park in March 1987, United winning 2-0 with goals by John Stiles and Micky Adams. How times have changed. Wigan were then in the old Division 3, while United were in Division 2 and went on to reach the FA Cup semi-final. When Kevin Blackwell's Leeds visited the JJB Stadium in February, 2005, the teams were in the same division and Wigan won 3-0.

Jim Beglin

Age: 41.
Joined Leeds: From Liverpool on a 'free' in 1989. He hadn't played for two seasons prior to joining Leeds due to injury.
So why did we sign him? If we could keep him fit he was a quality player. He was worth the gamble.
Did it pay off? No.
Games: 21.
After Leeds: Plymouth and Blackburn (all on loan). In the end you couldn't give him away.
Retired: 1991.
Did he give his body to science? He gave his voice to

broadcasting. He had plenty of time for local radio work during those long spells out through injury. He sought Howard Wilkinson's advice on what to do on retirement and it was Wilko who suggested the media.
So did he go straight into broadcasting? He tried a bit of coaching first but even the lightest work on the training ground left Jim needing buckets of ice to reduce the swelling in his knee. That is when his Leeds connection came up trumps.
Who was that? Rising star commentator Peter Drury knew Beglin from his Radio Leeds days. Beglin had a reputation for being approachable and talking sense. When Drury made the grade at national level with ITV and Radio 5, Jim went with him.
Did he get pigeon-holed? Irish radio used him for obvious reasons but Leeds were in the Premier League so appearances on TV began to increase. Who better to add the pro view of a Leeds game than a former player.
What about his homework. Does he do any? There's not as much prep work as the commentators, but you have to know about tactics and what a manager might be thinking.
Any Coleman's Balls? *"I was here at Maine Road when City lost 4-0 to Wimbledon, but they could have been 2-0 up after five minutes, and if they had been, the final score might just have been different."*
Hero: Johnny Giles, who knows the game inside out and Jim is still learning from him.
Relaxing: Plays golf off a handicap of five.

Rod Belfitt

Age: 60.
Leeds Era: 1963-1971.
Signed from: Retford Town aged 18.
A bit late: It was in the days when people left school aged seven to go down t'pit. Rod actually trained as a draughtsman before turning pro.
Games: 128 (33 goals).
Position: Striker.
On-field role: Target man.
Rod on modern day football: *"They don't know they're born. I remember playing four games in seven days and one of them was in Italy".* You tell 'em Rod.

Did they have to walk home in bare feet and get to Elland Road in time for the next game? It wasn't that bad but Rod's from the old school if you hadn't already gathered. If he hadn't been playing for Leeds he'd have been sweeping chimney stacks, except for the fact that he was a trained draughtsman.
Other clubs: Ipswich, Everton, Sunderland, Fulham (loan) and Huddersfield Town.
Retired: 1976.
So I guess he had something to fall back on after football? He went back to being a draughtsman for ten years.
But not longer? In 1986 he had a career change and entered the world of personal finance.
Oh dear: The next fifteen years were spent balancing books and selling pension plans. He gained lots more satisfaction from that than being at a drawing board all day.
And he had a brief spell with the taxman? He worked for the Inland Revenue in their valuation department. He wangled so much time off to play for the Inland Revenue football team that he only worked a few days a week.
Why did he leave his job as a financial adviser? Exams and courses became too 'taxing'. It's a young man's game so he retired in 2001 but Rod reckons there's no substitute for experience in any job.
Does he keep in touch with any of the Revie boys? Mainly Mick Bates and they both still play golf together.
Lives: Ackworth, S. Yorkshire.

Noel Blake

Age: 43.
Appearance: Darth Vadar in football boots.
Era: 1988-1990.
High point at Leeds: Captaining the side. His first game in charge was against Notts Forest in the FA Cup in 1989. Leeds lost 2-0.
Games: 51.
Position: Defender.
Kop chant: Bruno! Bruno!
Was he a clogger? Noel was an intelligent player. What he lacked in pace he made up for in brain matter.

How do you figure that one out? Whilst playing football he also studied to be a geography teacher.
Was the subject of any use as a player? It helped him find his way around the country and all the other clubs he played for.
Like? Aston Villa, Shrewsbury, Birmingham, Portsmouth, Stoke, Bradford, Dundee and finally Exeter.
Retired: 2001. He then became the Exeter manager. He got the job after being player/coach the season before.
How long did it last? 18 months. In 2002 Noel resigned and went into teaching. He was disillusioned with the game.
I guess the players didn't like all the homework he was giving them. Where did he teach? In the Staffordshire area but pupils at Longton High School always had their homework in on time. Or else! He taught PE too.
I suppose he prefers 'terms' to 'seasons': Hardly. In 2003 he was back in football as lst team coach at Notts County. He then went to Barnsley as assistant to Gudjon Thordarson and then back into teaching after Barnsley 'let him go' in 2004.
So he's a teacher again? Actually he's back in football at Stoke City but he says it's like being a teacher.
They both get 8 weeks off in the summer: He's now the Academy Manager with the tough task of training the youngsters. He decides who they sign and those they don't
Hobbies: Reading.

Billy Bremner

Born: Stirling, 1942.
Games: 742 (115 goals).
Position: Captain, midfield.
Leeds era: 60s and 70s.
Icon position: Number 1.
Reputation: A short fuse and a fierce competitor.
Left Leeds: Sold by Jimmy Armfield in 1976.
Other clubs: Hull City (1976-1978), Doncaster Rovers (1979-1982).
Retirement: 1982.

A player of Billy's stature doesn't leave the game to go into insurance does he? Billy took up the reigns at Doncaster.
Was he any good? Doncaster were in dire straits when he joined and he steered them out of the lowest division which was a feat in itself.
The ultimate job in football: In 1985 Billy was given his dream job of managing Leeds United. He was a victim of the success he had as a player and failed (by a whisker) to get Leeds out of the old Division 2.
When was he sacked? 1988. He never worked in football again. He tried his hand as a soccer pundit but never made the grade.
So where did he earn his money? His retirement coincided with a big demand for ex-players on the after-dinner circuit and he established himself as one of its big attractions.
Alex Ferguson on Billy: *"Billy would have walked into any side in the world both then and now."*
Billy on Billy: *"I was always considerate of my opponents. I used to dab iodine on my studs to avoid infection."*
Further reading: 'The Legend of Billy Bremner' and 'Billy: Pocket Book Hero'.
Legend has it: On away matches he would carry his socks in a Kellogg's corn flakes packet.
Allan Clarke on Billy: *"He was like a brother to me."*
Liked: Golf and a drink and a smoke. He also liked playing cards and dominoes.

Billy Bremner passed away 7th December 1997.

Tomas Brolin

Age: Still only 36.
Leeds era: 15 stone to 21 stone.
Came to Leeds with: Sparkling international credentials, a top level Italian pedigree...oh, and an injury. He had been Swedish footballer of the year in 1990 and 1994.
Left with: Reputation in ruins but much richer.
Cost: £4.5 million.
Games: 19.
George Graham on Brolin:
"I don't know where Tomas is. I would call his mobile but nobody at the club has his number."

After Leeds: Italy via Switzerland before turning up at Crystal Palace but made just 13 appearances.
Retired: 1998.
He could always set up a Swedish massage parlour: He did a summer of coaching on the east coast of America before returning home to Stockholm. In 1999 he turned out as goalkeeper for local Division 3 team Hudiksvallas ABK but only lasted one game.
So was finding work a problem? Not with a wealthy father who runs a property business. Tomas signed up and is very much part of the wheeler-dealer scene of Stockholm's property boom.
Not short of a few Krona: He is also the co-owner of a restaurant called 'Undici' – which means "11" in Italian (his shirt number at Parma). As you might guess it serves big portions. It is the place to be seen and at night becomes a hotspot for local celebrities. There is a dress code so no Leeds scarves.
Where seen? You can spot him on the internet selling his own range of shoes. Each pair has 'Brolin' inscribed on the side and the styles are named after Italian cities - can I have a pair of Rimini's size 7 please? Do you do the Napoli with velcro straps? He also has a share in a troubled business producing components for vacuum cleaners.
Wife: She's a former Miss Sweden and they have one child.
Hobbies: Trotting. Tomas owns the world's fastest trotter called 'Power to Charm'.

Tony Brown

Age: 47.
Leeds Era: 1982-1985.
Position: Centre back.
Goals: 1 against Shrewsbury.
Games: 24.
Leeds high point: Against Newcastle when he marked Kevin Keegan.
Aka: Tony the Tache or TB.
Retired: 1993 at Rochdale (he made over 100 appearances for the club). He also had a hernia and was the wrong side of 35 so his mind was made up.
Other clubs: Doncaster and Scunthorpe.

And so to the real world: After taking 1994 off to be a house husband Tony entered the world of insurance, working for a company called Royal London in Leeds.
What type of insurance? Life insurance, knocking door-to-door. He saw the job advertised in the newspaper and applied. He had no previous experience but managed okay.
Any amateur football? In 1996 he was playing for Bradford Park Avenue. A big fan of the team at the time was local businessman Jack Pennington who offered Tony a job.
Doing what? Selling power tools. He's the power tools king. Pennington's are based in Shipley and are industrial merchants to the trade. They sell nuts and bolts, electrical cabling – the sort of things you and me might need in an emergency.
What does Tony do? He's Customer Services Manager and has been there for almost 10 years. When you call the company, he's the guy who answers the phone.
What does he sound like? Like you wouldn't want to mess with him. Quite nasally with a broad Yorkshire accent. He's probably as hard as the nails they sell.
Does he still have the moustache? No. On a football trip to Dublin with players from Eccleshill United (a team he managed from 2002-2004) they held him down and shaved it off. It had been with him since he was 15.
How does he relax? Watching his two boys play football.
Lives: Bradford.

John Buckley

Age: 43.
Leeds era: 1986-1987.
Position: Left wing.
Games: 11 (1 goal - against Reading in September 1986).
Weaknesses: He was so tricky out on the wing that he often tricked himself.
In the Leeds book of lists: John would appear as left-winger in the worst Leeds team ever. A bit harsh possibly.
After Leeds: Leicester (loan), Rotherham, Scunthorpe, Partick Thistle and back to Rotherham.
Retired from playing: 1993.
Why? During a game in 1993

he went up for a header and very nearly never got up again. He'd fractured his skull in a clash of heads.
Sounds serious? John spent 18 months recuperating with weekly visits to brain specialists 'Headway' to help his physical and neurological recovery.
Was he all right? Yes though for two years he was unable to work. He did manage to pass his football coaching badges in that time.
This sounds like a charity appeal: Rotherham offered him a job as Community Officer in 1995. Then Leeds Academy took him on part-time and he worked his magic with the Under-12 team that included James Milner.
And after that? In 1999 he was on the move and worked as a fitness instructor in Doncaster as well as coaching Under-16s at Scunthorpe United. Then on to Hull City with the youth team.
Nowadays? Still coaching, but since 2003 his main role is managing the famous ladies' team, Doncaster Belles. He beat off stiff opposition from the Australian national coach.
I bet he did: They were the top ladies side a few years ago but are having a difficult 2005 season. In a recent match one of their strikers was sent off for taking her top off.
John on coaching: *"It's what you can do, not what you can't."*
Hobbies? Probably as a result of the accident, John has a very positive and philosophical attitude to living. He has a brilliant life and he loves spending time with Diane and two kids.

Kenny Burns

Age: 52.
Era: 1981-1984.
Looks like: A blonde, over-weight Sylvester Stallone.
Position: Defence.
Strengths: Hard as nails, good tackler.
Main weakness: Pace. He was so slow paint used to watch him dry.

He couldn't have been that slow, after all he won a European Cup winners medal and was 'Player of the Year' in 1978: He was carrying a few pounds when Allan Clarke signed him in 1981.
Other clubs: Birmingham, Notts Forest, Derby County, Notts County and finally Barnsley.
Retirement: In 1986 due to *"lack of pace"*.
And so into the real world: He went into the rag trade.
Was he a bouncer at Burton's? In 1987 he opened his own ladies boutique in Derby. It was Italian high fashion and very exclusive. Roughly translated the shop was called 'Posh Lady'.
Does Kenny admit to having a feminine side? It was his wife who ran the business. Kenny was more behind the scenes.
Suits you, sir: The shop's gross profit margin wasn't enough so after 3 years they flogged it.
Pity: In 1993 Kenny bought *The Blacksmith's Arms* in Uttoxeter. It served pints to farmers who knew nothing about football.
A good old-fashioned footballer's job: Kenny enjoyed it but in 1995 sold it to work for a Derby company called Manor House Furnishings. They supplied accessories to the caravan trade.
What did he do? Sales. In 1999 he began selling nick-nacks for a company called Minster Giftware. That didn't last long and he has since relied on corporate match day entertainment at Forest. He also has a radio phone-in on Century FM and does after-dinner speaking 2-3 times a month.
Hobbies? Apart from polishing his collection of shin-pads, he plays golf regularly.
Would we recognise him today: There's more hair on the front tyre of a jumbo jet but he still has the 'tache.

Burton

Born: 1900.

Origin: Some penniless Lithuanian peasant opened the first Burton shop in Chesterfield and today there are over 2,500 stores across the UK in many guises. They do clothes for fat people, trendy people, small people, women, and men and in 1998 changed their name to the Arcadia group.

So why are we featuring Burton's? They had the most appearances for Leeds as official shirt sponsors.

When? 1986-1989. After that they bunged one of their brands on the shirts (Top Man) for another two years.

Shouldn't Leeds have gone for something classier, like Millets or Mr Buyrite? The overriding factor was that Burton's had a big Leeds fan working for them at the time.

Was it the dashing Peter Ridsdale? He was on the board at Burton's and negotiated the deal with Leeds in 1985. For the next five years they sponsored the team with Rizza joining the Leeds board in 1987.

Any conflict of interests? Only from the players who had to wear Burton suits on match days.

Who was the club's first sponsor? RF Winder in 1982.

What did they do? They were into electrical switchgear and business transformers.

Did it enhance the company's name and image? Leeds were a second rate bunch with some distinctly average personnel but that didn't rub off on the company. They are still going strong and a lot of their trading came off the back of their association with Leeds United.

How did the first deal come about? Bill Fotherby saw what other clubs were doing and said I'll have some of that. It allowed the club to spend a bit more money on quality players like Frank Worthington and George McCluskey.

Go on then, list all the other sponsors: WGK, Lion Cabinets, Yorkshire Evening Post, Admiral, Thistle Hotels, Packard Bell, Strongbow, and Whyte & Mackay.

Aidan Butterworth

Age: 44.
Style: He could puff out his chest and run quickly at the same time. The result was goals. He wasn't the tallest but made up for it in effort.
Period: 1980-1984.
Top scorer: The 1983/84 season with 11 goals.
Only 11? It was in the days before Viagra when our attack was not very potent.
Games: 74.
Other clubs: Doncaster Rovers.
Butterworth on Butterworth: *"I soon realised I lacked the ability to be a top class footballer."*

Retired: 1986 aged just 25. Part injury, part disillusionment.
What next? Aidan had the brainpower to go back to college (Carnegie, Leeds) and did a 3-year degree in Human Movement Studies.
Where did that take him? Australia. His father lived out there and Aidan went for six months before returning to take a job in the Midlands buying and selling non-ferrous metals.
When was his big break? In 1994 PFA chief executive Gordon Taylor had seen Aidan's CV and put it forward for a job with Adidas in their marketing department. In 10 years at Adidas he worked up to the position of Sports Marketing Manager.
What did he do? He looked after Predator and David Beckham. Aidan was responsible for the Beckham/Jonny Wilkinson advertisement. He also organised a scouting system to get talented youngsters to wear Adidas booties.
Sounds like indoctrination? The parents would receive expenses and Adidas would treat their kids as well as any big club. Aidan says if they wear Adidas at 14 and make it, they will wear them right through their careers.
Sounds like a great job? It was and Aidan enjoyed his time there but he went freelance in 2004 to set up his own sports consultancy business based in York. Currently Puma was the only brand he could tell me about but watch this space.
Hobbies: Golf.
Lives: York.

Eric Cantona

Age: 39.

Appearance: A cross between Henry Winkler and Keith Moon.

Background: Bad boy of French soccer.

Leeds tally: 34 games (11 goals).

Wilkinson on Cantona: *"Eric likes to do what he likes, when he likes because he likes it – and then f***s off."*

Left Leeds: 26 November 1992.

Retired: 18 May 1997.

Any money worries? Cantona was loved by Nike. Celebrity status plus advertising revenue equals more cash than you could

fit on a team bus. It allowed him to pursue his main love of acting.

I've not seen him accepting any Oscars or did he send his sardines to pick them up? He's more art house than Hollywood and has been described as a film bore.

What films are we talking about here? He's made 8 in total from *Bonheur est dans le pre* ('Happiness in Field') in 1995 to *Clefs de bagnole* ('Car Keys') in 2003. His most famous role was in 'Elizabeth' playing Monsieur de Foix. He acted in the same scene with Cate Blanchett and dear, dear Dickie Attenborough.

Cantona on acting: *"On a film set, I try to empty my head, drift off into surrealist thoughts."*

What about directing? He is currently working on his second film as director with a feature about paranoia.

Maybe he should direct a film about his most famous moment in British football. Who would be cast to play Eric? Jackie Chan.

Most likely to be seen: At the beach. With his brother Joel they promote world beach football. Brazil plays host to the 2005 Beach World Cup and all the promotional literature has Eric featured on the front.

That must be worth something: Eric says he gets nothing out of it other than enjoyment. He's been playing since 1995.

Will Eric be representing France? Possibly. It's a 5-a-side game and his brother is team manager.

Hobbies: Shooting, philosophy, poetry, painting.

Aidan Butterworth

Age: 44.
Style: He could puff out his chest and run quickly at the same time. The result was goals. He wasn't the tallest but made up for it in effort.
Period: 1980-1984.
Top scorer: The 1983/84 season with 11 goals.
Only 11? It was in the days before Viagra when our attack was not very potent.
Games: 74.
Other clubs: Doncaster Rovers.
Butterworth on Butterworth:
"I soon realised I lacked the ability to be a top class footballer."

Retired: 1986 aged just 25. Part injury, part disillusionment.
What next? Aidan had the brainpower to go back to college (Carnegie, Leeds) and did a 3-year degree in Human Movement Studies.
Where did that take him? Australia. His father lived out there and Aidan went for six months before returning to take a job in the Midlands buying and selling non-ferrous metals.
When was his big break? In 1994 PFA chief executive Gordon Taylor had seen Aidan's CV and put it forward for a job with Adidas in their marketing department. In 10 years at Adidas he worked up to the position of Sports Marketing Manager.
What did he do? He looked after Predator and David Beckham. Aidan was responsible for the Beckham/Jonny Wilkinson advertisement. He also organised a scouting system to get talented youngsters to wear Adidas booties.
Sounds like indoctrination? The parents would receive expenses and Adidas would treat their kids as well as any big club. Aidan says if they wear Adidas at 14 and make it, they will wear them right through their careers.
Sounds like a great job? It was and Aidan enjoyed his time there but he went freelance in 2004 to set up his own sports consultancy business based in York. Currently Puma was the only brand he could tell me about but watch this space.
Hobbies: Golf.
Lives: York.

Eric Cantona

Age: 39.
Appearance: A cross between Henry Winkler and Keith Moon.
Background: Bad boy of French soccer.
Leeds tally: 34 games (11 goals).
Wilkinson on Cantona: *"Eric likes to do what he likes, when he likes because he likes it – and then f***s off."*
Left Leeds: 26 November 1992.
Retired: 18 May 1997.
Any money worries? Cantona was loved by Nike. Celebrity status plus advertising revenue equals more cash than you could

fit on a team bus. It allowed him to pursue his main love of acting.
I've not seen him accepting any Oscars or did he send his sardines to pick them up? He's more art house than Hollywood and has been described as a film bore.
What films are we talking about here? He's made 8 in total from *Bonheur est dans le pre* ('Happiness in Field') in 1995 to *Clefs de bagnole* ('Car Keys') in 2003. His most famous role was in 'Elizabeth' playing Monsieur de Foix. He acted in the same scene with Cate Blanchett and dear, dear Dickie Attenborough.
Cantona on acting: *"On a film set, I try to empty my head, drift off into surrealist thoughts."*
What about directing? He is currently working on his second film as director with a feature about paranoia.
Maybe he should direct a film about his most famous moment in British football. Who would be cast to play Eric? Jackie Chan.
Most likely to be seen: At the beach. With his brother Joel they promote world beach football. Brazil plays host to the 2005 Beach World Cup and all the promotional literature has Eric featured on the front.
That must be worth something: Eric says he gets nothing out of it other than enjoyment. He's been playing since 1995.
Will Eric be representing France? Possibly. It's a 5-a-side game and his brother is team manager.
Hobbies: Shooting, philosophy, poetry, painting.

Brian Caswell

Age: 49.
Era: 1985-1988.
Accent: Brummie.
Position: Left back.
Games: 9.
Treatment table: Yet another Leeds player who spent more time on the injury list than actually playing.
Brought to Leeds by: Billy Bremner.
The sad news is: Brian is another candidate to play at the back in Leeds' worst ever team.
Other clubs: Walsall, Doncaster and Wolverhampton.
Retired: In 1988 on doctors orders.

Did he get a second opinion? If he had been a horse he would have been put down. The injury that cost him his career came in his very first game for his new club, Wolverhampton – since he was on loan from Leeds they just sent him back to Elland Road. He used to travel with his own treatment table.
So Leeds got him back? Yes and whilst recuperating, Brian earned his coaching badge and got a job as a coach in Birmingham's Football in the Community scheme.
Didn't dodgy knees affect his ability to do the job? If anything it enhanced his role since he had to look at coaching from a different angle.
From a wheelchair? Not exactly. He is mobile but more Nicky Campbell than Darren Campbell. Anyway, he got promoted to youth team coach and then did much of the same in 1992 at Stoke City. He was assistant manager to Wayne Clarke at Telford for 2 years in 1995 and was back as youth team coach at Northampton and then Shrewsbury until 2002.
Don't tell me the youth scene dried up? Seemingly. Today Brian is working for BMW in the Midlands. He's in customer services. He makes buying a Beemer quite painless.
Brian on BMW: *"They stay together better than my body ever did."*
Hobbies: Golf.
Lives: Walsall where he is still a legend.

Jeff Chandler

Age: 46.
Appearance: A cross between a hobbit and Jim Kerr.
Not to be confused with: Jeff Chandler, the Hollywood western actor.
Era: 1979-1981.
Bought by: Jimmy Adamson.
Games: 28 (2 goals).
Position: Left midfield.
Money, money, money: When Allan Clarke took over as manager, Jeff had put a down payment on a house in Leeds (he previously commuted to Elland Road from the Lancashire Riviera). Clarkey promptly sold

him to Bolton and Jeff lost his £5,000 deposit.
Retired: 1991 at Cardiff.
Reason: Injury.
Then down the job centre? Hardly. Jeff began selling double-glazing, door-to-door in Blackpool.
Not a bad place to start with all that rain and wind: It went well at first but he then began working with an agency selling advertising. That lasted 4 years and in 1995 he started up his own business selling Range Rovers.
Called? Furlong Motors. It was during this period that Jeff agreed to do some voluntary social work. He enjoyed it so much that in 1997 he became a full-time social worker.
What happened to the Range Rovers? They financially failed their MOTs if you get my drift.
Don't you have to be qualified to be a social worker? It's 3 years of wearing dungarees and passing exams but he qualified in 2001.
So what is he? In 2002 he became a Youth Justice Worker, part of the youth offending team in Preston. He makes sure ASBO's are enforced and naughty boys under the age of 17 are doing their community orders.
He's a sort of PC Plod to Toytown's Sly and Gobbo? It's hard work but as rewarding as scoring goals.
How does he relax? Eating out.
Family: Wife and 2 daughters, 20 and 17.
Lives: Blackpool from where his wife originates.

Lee Chapman

Age: 46.
Appearance: Expelled PE teacher at a posh private school.
First wage: £40 per week at Stoke City.
Leeds era: 1990-1993. He also played 2 games in 1996.
Forte: Getting the ball into the net using his head.
Goal celebration: He would attempt to glide back to his own half like an oil slick damaged cormorant.
Games: 172 (80 goals).
Retired: 1996 at Swansea City.
Action man: Lee took his talents to London in 1997 when

he opened the trendy bar and restaurant called 'Teatro'.
Didn't he open one in Leeds, too? Sshhh! In 2000 Leeds Teatro did open and then closed again. Leeds United invested heavily and lost their 25% stake when it shut its doors less than a year later.
I went there once and they charged me a fiver for a drink: Maybe that's why it didn't last. This is Leeds not London.
What about the bar in London? They did very nice food but Teatro ran into financial difficulties in 2002. After a re-invention and a name change (SOUK) it was sold in November 2004. Lee claims the whole market for posh dining has fallen by the way-side in favour of more relaxed and social grazing.
I missed that in the papers: The press are more interested in his private life with 'er indoors, Lesley Ash. She currently has the MRSA virus but is better known for acting and lip opera-tions.
Another double act: What made Lee such a favourite at Leeds was his partnership with Rod Wallace. You just have to look at Lee's strike rate to see how well the Wallace/Chapman partner-ship got on.
Still in demand: Lee recently turned down £100,000 for one week's work in the 'Big Brother' household.
Let's stick to football: He was quality at Leeds.
Currently: Chappie and his wife run a small bar in Clapham.
Hobbies: Wine and suing the medical profession.

Jack Charlton

Age: 70.
Leeds era: 1951-1973.
1951! Hanging was still in operation: He's the oldest player we feature.
Games: 762 (94 goals). He holds the club's appearance record. He regularly played 50 games a season.
Position: Centre half.
One club man: He only ever played for Leeds United.

Other clubs (as manager): Middlesbrough, Sheffield Wednesday, Newcastle, also Republic of Ireland - his hobby in those days was scanning players' passports to see if they had any Irish blood in them.
Medals: He has a World Cup winners medal plus a 1972 FA Cup winners medal which he got at the age of 37...among others.
TV Ads: Shredded Wheat.
Management retirement: 1996. To fill the gap he extended his TV and after-dinner appearances.
Relaxation: He is still seen in both roles but spends as much time as possible nowadays with wife Pat and the rest of the family. Jack enjoys country pursuits, especially fishing, and a little known fact is that he's adept at woodwork.
If he ever gets thirsty: Jack can pop back to Dublin. He was given the freedom of the city after 1996 World Cup and so gets his Guinness for free.
Superstitious: Jack is well known for his superstitions. He gave up the Leeds captaincy because he wanted to be last out of the tunnel.
In contact: He still meets up with his Leeds team-mates from the Revie era, though at 70 he is the 'grand old man' of the group. Once described as "a one man awkward squad", Jack still has forthright views that he is not afraid to express.
What does Big Jack think of the EU Constitution? They'll never win the Champions League.
Shopkeeper: During Jack's spell as Middlesbrough manager, he and Pat were in charge of the club shop. Can you imagine that happening these days?

Trevor Cherry

Age: 57.
Era: 1972-1982.
Position: Captain, midfielder and full back.
Previous club: Huddersfield Town.
Interestingly: He picked up more bookings in his first season with Leeds (9) than he did in the previous 8 seasons with Huddersfield.
Role: To fill the boots of an ageing Terry Cooper at full-back.
Other clubs: Bradford City.
Retired: 1985.
And straight into...? Management at Bradford. He

lasted five seasons but the Bradford fire changed everything and he was dismissed in 1990. He was offered the Sunderland job after Lawrie McMenemy resigned but he turned it down to develop his business interests.

Doing what? In 1990 he joined a small company called SLP. They specialised in promotional merchandising and had a big catalogue like Argos. Trevor increased the company's success and the business was sold to Conrad PLC in 1996. He also had interests in Taylor Made Sports, a corporate hospitality business which was also sold.

For megabucks? Trevor wouldn't say but whilst he was waiting for the cheque to clear he became a director of Huddersfield Town, a position he kept until 1999.

And for my next trick: Two years was spent playing golf. That was until he was enticed back into the world of company directorships. Not one but three companies hired his services.

And they are? Sellers Travel Agents, a property company and Taskcatch PLC - they specialise in indoor 5-a-side football.

Football seems to be a theme: As of 2005, Trevor has backed a company called Just Signatures and they do souvenir coins for Celtic and Rangers. The heads of famous ex-players adorn each coin.

Maybe Trevor should produce a coin for Leeds United. Instead of the Queen's head on the back it would have McQueen's head: There are no plans at the moment but Trevor is still a Leeds fan and goes to every home game.

Allan Clarke

Age: 59.
Looks like: James Bolam.
Aka: 'Sniffer'. He was like a pig finding truffles. Only Allan dug up something more precious.
You mean goals? He was a truly world class operator and England international.
Heaven sent: Allan believes he was put on this earth with a gift. That gift was to play football and thankfully God was a Leeds fan.
But he didn't just play for Leeds: No but his time at Leeds was his defining era. 1969-1978. He's still a hero and goes to most home games.

Retired: 1980. He managed Barnsley that same year and was the first of the Revie old boys to return to take charge at Elland Road.
With any success? Relegation is a dirty word in football. He was fired in 1982 but he did bring John Sheridan to the club.
And Peter Barnes: In 1983 he went to manage Scunthorpe but that didn't go too well and so he left to sell portakabins.
The obvious career move: In 1985 he had a second spell at Barnsley which lasted over 4 years. Eventually he was sacked and after a short stop-off at Lincoln City he quit football management for good after 12 years.
At least he had the portakabin business to fall back on: Allan remained unemployed for nearly 3 years after Lincoln. It was the low point of his life. Eventually in 1993, he had a call from the former Scunthorpe chairman who moved him from portakabins to set up a company called MTS Nationwide.
What did they do? Heavy plant hire to construction companies. Allan is a sales rep selling industrial fume extractors and wielding sets. He does talk football all day though.
Is he still there? 12 years on and Allan still enjoys the work.
You could write a book about all that: Allan did. In 2002 *Sniffer: The Life and Times of Allan Clarke* hit the shelves.
Controversial? He speaks his mind and has some great ries. He played with pleurisy during the FA Cup defeat against Colchester in 1971 but didn't know the extent of his illness until The Don told him as he was leaving the pitch at full-time.

Terry Connor

Age: 42.
Appearance: An 'Eastenders' extra.
Leeds era: 1979-1983.
Games: 108 (22 goals).
Position: Up front.
Debut: Came on as sub against WBA in 1979 and scored the winner.
Product: Of the Leeds schools footballing system. He went to Foxwood School for the sport not the 'O' levels.
Other clubs: Brighton, Portsmouth, Swansea City, and Bristol City (player/coach).
Retired: 1992.

The transition to backroom staff: Since a knee injury ended his playing career at Bristol City, Connor set off on his coaching career at both Bristol City and Bristol Rovers via a stint at Swindon Town as the club's coach in the community.

1999: Terry's boss at both Bristol clubs was offered a job as assistant manager at Wolves and took Terry with him. Terry is still there today and in charge of developing the club's young players who come out of the Academy.

Other duties: When his crystal ball is cloudy current manager Glenn Hoddle sends Terry to watch Wolves' future opponents and the 'master spy' compiles a dossier of their strengths and weaknesses. He ran the rule over his old club Leeds before Wolves' visit in 2004/2005.

'A soccer gardener': That's how Terry is best described. His biggest thrill is seeing his young talents flourish, grow and blossom into first team players. How ever much manure you throw at them, some still turn into weeds.

On the buses: Before he owned a car, the young Connor would catch a double decker bus from his home in Chapeltown to Elland Road and then play for the first team.

Late developer: Because he couldn't swim Terry was the butt of all jokes. He decided he couldn't have his children growing up unable to swim himself so he learned and managed enough strokes to get by. He can now be left to have a bath on his own.

Lives: Sutton Coldfield with wife Jan and three children.

Foxwood School: Closed down years ago and not before time.

Terry Cooper

Age: 61.
Looks like: Phil Collins.
Nickname: 'TC'.
Leeds era: Don Revie to Jimmy Armfield. 14 seasons in all.
Position: Left back or left wing.
Signature: His white boots. There was a kids version of the boot with a circular dial on the underside which allowed them to break their ankle more easily.
Games: 341 (goals 11).
Other clubs: Middlesbrough, Bristol City (player/manager/director), Bristol Rovers (player/coach), Doncaster Rovers (assisting Billy Bremner), Exeter

(manager), Birmingham (manager and director) and Southampton (assistant manager/scout).
Retired: 1985.
England caps: 20.
Best remembered for: The goal that gave Leeds their first major trophy, the League Cup, against Arsenal in 1968.
Present job: He's based out in Tenerife as Southampton's scout in Europe and South America.
Cushy: It's great if you enjoy travel. Terry had originally intended retiring to Tenerife but Graeme Souness offered him the assistant manager's job at Southampton. When Dave Jones took over he gave Terry the ideal opportunity to be based in Tenerife, scouting for European and South American players.
Retirement 2: Terry quit due to ill health in 1995, during his second spell as manager of Exeter, but he is now in good health and enjoys long walks while away on his scouting missions.
Any other jobs on the CV? In the late 70s during his spell at Middlesbrough (with beard) he also owned a newsagents shop.
Family life: Terry's son Mark is manager of Tamworth in the Nationwide Conference. Terry and his wife Rosemary also have two daughters and six grandchildren. One daughter lives in Tenerife and the other is an air-hostess with Monarch Airlines.
Revie Reunions: He would love to join in more of the get-togethers enjoyed by his team-mates from the Revie era, but the distance involved means he only rarely meets up with them these days.

Andy Couzens

Age: 30.
Era: 1993-1997.
First club: Leeds. He came up through the youth system with Woodgate, Kewell and Smith.
Position: Midfield.
High point: His full debut against Nottingham Forest in 1994.
Appearances: 35 (2 goals).
Shipping forecast: Andy left Leeds for Carlisle United in 1997 and then Blackpool in 1999.
Retired: At the end of the 2000 season aged just 25. There was no Pleasure Beach for Andy at Blackpool.

That's young: Andy figured he wasn't going to make the grade and spent the next 15 months unemployed, trying to get a job within the game.
As a player or a programme seller? He had trials with Barnet and Hartlepool and played some amateur stuff for Harrogate Town but no firm offers.
Sounds desperate: In 2001 Andy started training to become a fitness instructor. It was a 3-month intensive course with exams every Friday and by the end he was fully qualified and got a job.
Where? A close friend was the manager of the local Marriot leisure complex at Hollins Hall, Baildon. He offered Andy a job in the summer of 2001.
What did that involve? Getting people fitter, helping them lose weight. He had clients aged from 70 down to 18.
Is there a secret to losing weight? Become a professional footballer.
Was there a diet regime when he was at Leeds? No.
They say life is a treadmill: For Andy it is. In the autumn of 2002 he became self-employed as a personal trainer and still works out of Hollins Hall.
Married: No, but likes his golf and he plays a bit of badminton to county level.
He sounds like Mr Motivator: He has done some TV on a fitness show called 'Inside Out'.
Did that lead to anything? The end credits.

Tony Currie

Age: 55.
Born: London.
Appearance: A cross between the singer of a glam rock band and sea trawlerman.
Nickname: 'TC'.
Hang on, wasn't that Terry Cooper's nickname? Yes. Only one nickname was allowed in those days so they had to wait until Terry was sold before Tony could sign. UEFA regulations.
Era: 1976-1979
Games: 124 (16 goals).
International caps: Only 17. Shame on the FA.
Strengths: Creativity, pin-point passing and shooting.

Weaknesses: Pace, heading, injury prone and food.
Room-mate: Allan Clarke then Ray Hankin.
Rumour has it: Tony was invited to write for a gay magazine in Germany after himself and Leicester City's Alan Birchenall kissed during a match. That incident in 1975 also raised questions in the House of Commons.
An MP probably wanted his phone number. What happened after Leeds? QPR (1979-1983), Toronto Nationals and Torquay (1984-1985). Later he played non-league for Chesham, Hendon and Goole (as player/manager).
Retired: 1987 at Goole - that same year he had an operation to repair his left knee – it didn't work.
A man with his ability must have stayed in football: In 1988 Tony applied for the job as Football Community Officer at Sheffield United (his club before Leeds). He's been there ever since. He's now part of the furniture.
Duties: Coaching kids in schools, getting more people to watch the Blades, arranging tours of Bramall Lane, birthday parties.
Has he sat on the ball in the middle of a game recently? He still could do, but only in his office. Tony says he can't actually play football any more due to a chronic knee problem.
Hobbies: Golf, music, films/TV, most sports and holidays.
Favourite film: 'Where Eagles Dare'.
Leeds nutshell? He played the best football of his career with the best players, in front of the best fans.

Alan Curtis

Age: 51.
Aka: 'Alan Courteous' because he's such a nice guy.
Joined Leeds: 1979 from Swansea City.
Games: 35 (6 goals).
Position: Centre forward.
High point: Scoring a brace against Bristol City in his very first game.
Low point: Colliding with Peter Shilton against Forest and never being the same player again.
Used to live: Bramhope - a few doors down from Norman Hunter.
Clubs after Leeds: Swansea (again), Southampton, Sunderland, Cardiff and Swansea (again).
Retired: 1990.
First job: Schools Programme Officer for Swansea City.
Swansea aren't known for keeping anyone long: Remarkably, Curtis kept that job for 6 years. Managers are a different matter: Micky Adams, Jan Molby, John Hollins, Terry Yorath, Brian Flynn and Alan Cork all got the chop within 5 minutes of arriving at the club.
Were they all nice to Alan? Jan Molby promoted Curtis to youth team coach in 1996. When Molby was sacked in 1999, new manager Alan Cork promoted Curtis to assistant manager.
Oh dear, I can see what's coming: In 2001 Curtis was sacked along with manager at the time John Hollins.
So down the job centre? Afraid so. Alan took a job with Swansea based sports promotion company Bergoni selling football kits to schools. He also tried his hand at radio commentary and had a football phone-in on Real Radio.
So he's out of favour at Swansea, he's out of football, who employed him next? Swansea.
Alan and Swansea are like Siamese twins. I'll bet his favourite food is meat and two Vetch: In 2002 new boss John Cusack took Alan back on as assistant manager but when another new manager came in (Brian Flynn), Alan became the Head of Development where he is today. Flynny got the push in March 2004.

Bobby Davison

Age: 46.

Late starter: Bobby didn't turn pro until he was 21.

What was he doing before that? He worked on the shipyards in the Northeast.

Big break: A teacher encouraged him to write off to clubs for a trial. It paid off when Huddersfield signed him in 1980.

Leeds era: 1987-1992.

Position: Attacker.

Games: 110 (36 Goals).

A legend at: Derby County.

Pro ranks retirement: 1995 at Hull City.

I see some non-league action on the horizon: Bobby went to Guiseley as player/coach for two years before fully retiring at 40 in 1999.

No room at Elland Road? He fancied a job on the coaching side at Leeds but answered an advert for a coach with Bradford City and got the job.

All credit to the personnel department: Mr. D started out by coaching Bradford's Under-13s, and schoolkids in the holidays. It was a job he loved. Then an opportunity came along to coach the youth team.

Robson and Todd: When Bryan Robson and Colin Todd took charge in 2003 they asked Bobby to take over the reserves. Robson left in 2004 and Bobby became Todd's assistant.

Bobby D to Vinnie Jones: *"Do you know we pass to feet at this club?"*

Vinnie J to Bobby D: A smack in the mouth.

Any ambition to be a manager? As a footballer you want to be a first team player, so any ambitious coach wants to be a manager, although Bobby is happy learning his trade under Todd.

Home: After many years living in Burley in Wharfedale, Bobby and his wife have moved to an apartment in Ilkley.

Sounds like a retirement home: Bobby is very, very, very busy trying to help Bradders out of Division 1.

Favourite Charity: Motor Neurone Disease.

Mervyn Day

Age: 50.
Born: Chelmsford.
Leeds era: 1985-1993. He was an ever present under Bremner and Wilkinson until Leeds returned to Division 1.
Position: Goalkeeper.
Games: 268.
Time to move on: When Leeds re-signed John Lukic in 1990, Day only made 5 appearances in 3 years. It is not great on your CV.
Other clubs: West Ham, Leyton Orient, Aston Villa, Luton, Sheffield United and Carlisle.
Retired: 1994.
Leeds high point: Winning promotion at the end of the 1989/1990 season.
Low point: Attacked by Birmingham fans as he left the field at half-time in a 1-0 defeat at St. Andrew's in 1985.
Most famous for: Age 20, being the youngest keeper to play in an FA Cup Final (1975 for West Ham against Fulham).
Who came knocking on the door of opportunity? It was his former club Carlisle. They were in need of someone to manage the side when a dispute over a re-arranged game saw them relegated. The manager left and in stepped Merv who immediately got Carlisle back into Division 2 that next season.
So things are going well: Not entirely. Mervyn was relieved of his duties at the start of the 1997 season and a man in a suit (Michael Knighton) appointed himself as joint-manager.
Where did Day go? To Everton as a goalkeeping coach. Day is one of the most decorated of coaches so his talents were not going unnoticed. In 1998 he was poached to join Charlton Athletic as the first team coach – a position he still has. He shares his office with Glynn Snodin.
How is he coping with the pace of the Premiership? It is hard work but he loves working with players and getting them prepared.
Other business interests: Merv is a consultant for Eidos and endorses the Play Station computer game Championship Manager 5.
Lives: South-East London.

Ken De Mange

Age: 41.
Era: 1987-1988.
Sounds like: A stage name for a dodgy ventriloquism act.
Ken De who? Is he French? He's actually from Dublin. Get this, he even played for Ireland against the mighty Brazil.
I don't remember him: He played 20 times for Leeds.
I still don't remember him: He scored on his debut against Man City in just 7 minutes.

That Ken De Mange: He came to Leeds having been part of the Liverpool squad that won everything in the 80s.
He must have been good: He didn't actually get a game for Liverpool in the four years he was there, but he must have been good just to be a reserve.
So he had potential? Most definitely. He says his biggest regret in life was asking to leave Leeds in 1998.
Why did he do that? He only wanted a bigger slice of the 1st team action. Unfortunately Leeds had Sheridan, Strachan, Batty and Speed in his preferred midfield position.
Clubs after Leeds: Hull City and Cardiff (on loan).
Retired: 1991. He went back to live in Ireland and played amateur football for four different Irish clubs in 2 seasons. He quit all forms of football in 1993 due to a hip injury.
Then what happened? His partner lived in London and worked for British Airways as a stewardess, so Ken joined her in Kingston and applied for a job he had heard was available.
What job? Baggage handler at Heathrow Airport – Terminal One. He has been doing it since 1994. He mainly does the European and domestic flights and it's physical work but he enjoys the 'craic'.
I bet he gets cheap flights: Who needs air miles when you get your flights for nothing. Ken reckons he doesn't have time to take holidays since he has two young kiddies. The only time he gets time off is in the summer when there's a baggage handlers strike.
Hero: Johnny Giles. He had pictures of him on his bedroom wall as a kid.

Martin Dickinson

Age: 42.
Leeds era: 1980-1986.
Games: 119 (2 goals).
Position: Central defence and midfield.
Debut: Against Middlesbrough in 1980. He came on 18 days after his 17th birthday.

A product of the youth system: Martin and Terry Connor were the first Leeds-born players to progress into the senior side since Paul Madeley and David Harvey in the mid-60s.
Let go: After Eddie Gray was sacked, Billy Bremner did the deed. Surplus to requirements.
Other clubs: West Brom and Sheffield United.
Retired: 1989.
Reason: Martin was a regular motorway user during his spell at Sheffield United. He was hit from behind by a van and suffered whiplash injuries when his own car hit a crash barrier.
How bad was it? His neck was weakened so badly that he had to retire from football and waited five years for the insurance payout from the accident. He played just one game for Sheffield United. He was only 26.
What happened next? He started a laundry business that folded but now he's usually up a ladder. He runs a window cleaning business in South Anston, Sheffield, with his son Joe.
Any confessions? Plenty. Many a time customers have stepped out of the shower without knowing Martin was washing the windows and he's been given a full frontal flash.
What a carry on: He's also seen neighbours entering someone else's house and coming out with wet hair and a huge grin!
What does he do when he's not cleaning windows? Martin enjoys watching horse racing and having a bet. Peter Scudamore is a close friend.
So he gets some good tips? Don't bet on it. His main love is pigeons though.
Fancy that: He actually breeds racing pigeons for his Dad and Uncle. They are top quality pigeons and win plenty of cash. Martin used to race his own birds but now breeds them in lofts in his back garden.

John Donnelly

Age: 44.
Born: Glasgow.
Lookalike: Kevin Rowland, front man of Dexy's Midnight Runners.
Leeds era: 1982-1985.
I've not really heard of him: You should have. When Eddie Gray signed him he said he was the best player in the country. When Eddie heard we'd contacted John, the former Leeds manager was on the phone asking for his telephone number. John wasn't easy to track down.

Games: 44 (4 goals).
So what happened? Therein lies another story. John didn't want to go into details about why he quit football at such an early age. Let's say he became fed up with the game.
Lived: Beeston.
Leeds room-mate: Martin Dickinson.
Other clubs: Motherwell, Dumbarton, Partick and Dunfermline. By accounts he had a few scrapes with all his former employers.
Retired: 1988 aged just 28.
What is he known as today? The Mother Theresa of boys football. From 1988 until the present time John has dedicated himself to working and coaching kids of all ages in Glasgow.
That's very noble: Until 1993 he was working for the Scottish FA and now an organisation that nurtures young talent in the East End of Glasgow. He's has had boys who have gone on to become pros at Aberdeen, Celtic and Kilmarnock. He even coached Glasgow's Leeds United boys club.
Does he keep in contact with any of the old boys? It's been 20 years since he left Leeds and has had no contact with any of his former team-mates. He sees George McCluskey in his cab sometimes but admits he wouldn't get a free ride. The former Leeds player John McGoldrick went to his 40th birthday party but meetings are rare.
Hobbies: Horse racing. He likes a bet and follows the form.
A chip off the old block: He has one son also called John who is currently on the books of Partick Thistle.

Tony Dorigo

Age: 40.
Born: Melbourne.
Leeds era: 1991-1997.
Games: 208 (5 goals).
Other clubs: Aston Villa, Chelsea, Torino, Derby and Stoke.
Style: More one footed than Don Brennan.
Hedging his bets: When it comes to sport, Tony has a real problem over who to support. He's the Australian-born son of an Italian, won 11 England caps, had a spell playing for Torino in Italy and has business interests in Portugal.

Master of all trades: While still playing for his last club, Stoke City, Tony ran a vehicle leasing company called *Premier Vehicles*. He sold that in 2003 to devote more time to property development while still doing a considerable amount of TV and radio work as a football analyst. Tony bought a few properties as an investment and soon saw it as a profitable business. An opportunity arose in Portugal and in 2002 he started a property development company, Premiership Developments, which is now thriving.

He didn't fancy taking over The Dog and Duck? Not on your life. He always wanted to do something different because it's a big world out there. Currently his company is developing a 100 unit apartment site in Carvoeiro in the Algarve, and there are two more projects in the pipeline including 220 units with a golf course and hotel development and a very large 700 unit development.

How does a footballer succeed in the property business? It's been a big learning curve, but good lawyers and accountants have helped him build his expertise. In the first year you spend a lot of money and try not to make too many mistakes. The first development was in a prime site, and since then the business has really taken off, and Tony hardly has a minute to spare. The company can even sell units straight off the plans, before a brick has been laid.

Lives: Hartford, Cheshire, with wife Heather and three kids. He also has a place in Portugal.

Keith Edwards

Age: 47.

Leeds era: 1986-1987.

Games: 50 (9 goals). He actually stockpiled 256 league goals over his career.

Goal ratio: Keith's hit rate was terrific until he came to Leeds. When he left he began scoring for fun again. Strange that.

Best remembered for: The header he scored after leaving the bench in the FA Cup semi-final defeat against Coventry at Hillsborough in 1987 to take the game into extra time.

Edwards on Bremner, the manager: *"Billy didn't have his players practising corners or free kicks because he believed if you couldn't already deliver a good set piece you shouldn't be a footballer."*

Other clubs: Sheffield United (twice), Hull City (twice), Aberdeen, Stockport, Huddersfield Town and Plymouth (loan).

Retired: 1990.

Getting tankered up: After quitting the game, he spent eighteen months reducing his golf handicap. Then Joe Bolton, who had played for Sheffield United, got him into tanker driving, and transporting hazardous chemicals around the country.

Did he eat Yorkie bars? He got his HGV license and had a tab at over a dozen transport cafes. You drink tea out of mugs not cups.

But what about his love of the game? Cabin life was not for Keith since he didn't enjoy the days away from home.

So what's on the agenda these days? Work, he reckons, is over-rated! He is much happier combining fund raising for Cancer Research UK with working for BBC Radio Sheffield and Radio Humberside.

Local derby: The Blades' Yorkshire derby at Leeds in April 2005 brought Keith back to Elland Road in his radio role for the first time since being sold to Aberdeen in 1987.

Hobbies: He enjoys going to the Cheltenham Festival every year, mixing his time between racing and golf. He likes going to the greyhounds too and doing after-dinner engagements.

Family: Single parent Keith has a son and three daughters.

Roger Eli

Age: 39.

Leeds era: 1982-1985.

Debut: Blink and you'll have missed it. He came on as sub against Wimbledon in 1984.

Games: 2.

Not much in 3 years: Leeds was his first club so he was still learning the ropes.

Did he go on to bigger and better things? That's for you to decide but here's the list - Wolves, Cambridge, Crewe, Pontefract Collieries, York City, Bury, Northwich, Burnley, Scarborough, Scunthorpe, Partick, Farsley Celtic, and Otley Town (player/manager).

Heroes: Peter Lorimer and Eddie Gray. They were the David Beckhams of their day – brilliantly gifted players.

Life after Leeds: His five-year term at Turf Moor was the most productive of his career. He had played in central defence and midfield at Leeds but took his chance up front at Burnley.

The Chinese way: At 5ft 11in Eli was small for a central defender but during his season with Foshan, in the Chinese first division, it was a pleasant change for him to be the tallest!

Roger the businessman: After retiring from league football in 1995, he set up a textile business as an agent, exporting cloth. After ten years he switched to his present job - selling corporate gifts for catalogue companies. When an insurance company offers gifts as an incentive for taking out one of its policies, he provides the gifts.

The very latest: Just before our interview, Roger quit as player/manager of Otley Town in the West Riding County Amateur League. He had held the post for a year but suspected his ambitions were not quite matched by some people at the club.

Were games cancelled due to the pitch being double booked with a local Morris dancing association? You must remember Roger only wanted the best for the club. Subsequently, just after our interview he rejoined Otley Town as manager for the 2005/2006 season.

Lives: Clayton, Bradford, with wife Andrea and son Jordan, aged three and a half.

Roy Ellam

Age: 62.
Position: Central defender.
Appearance: Overgrown space alien.
Era: 1972-1974.
Role: To fill the gap between the retirement of Jack Charlton and the arrival of Gordon McQueen.
1st pay packet: £150. Not bad.
Previous clubs: Bradford and Huddersfield.
After Leeds: Huddersfield.
America beckons: In 1975 Roy set his stall out on the US pro-circuit playing for Philadelphia and Washington.
Any famous team-mates? No

but he played against Pele five times. He said he was the *"only player who marked me out of the game when it was my job to mark him out of the game."*

Then what happened? Injury forced Roy back to the UK in 1976 where he began a career selling garden compost for Sinclair Horticulture.

How long did it last? Compost was where it was at. After 7 stinking years Roy got into the pub game.

Ah, a proper profession: The Whitbread's owned *Nelson* in Dewsbury put Roy in charge as landlord for 10 years from 1983-1993. He moved to *The Red Lion* in Barnsley for 12 months and then bought his own boozer called *The Gate* in 1994.

Who were his regulars? Bremner, Giles, Lorimer.

Did he run a quiz night? Quizzes, darts, pool, big screen...he said he loved it.

No sign of retirement? He sold the pub in 2002 and moved to Barnsley.

It sounds like good business? He used the money to help finance his daughter's fitness centre in Dewsbury.

What is it called? Fitness Connection. He does gym inductions and the over 65s can join in one of Roy's classes.

Pumping zimmer frames? He's dedicated to helping out and donates the rest of his spare time to looking after his grandchildren.

How does he remember his time at Leeds? It was Christmas Day every day.

Wayne Entwhistle

Age: 47.
Leeds era: 1979-1980.
Position: Forward.
Role: To put himself about a bit.
Games: 12 (2 goals).
Entwhistle on Entwhistle: *"I wasn't good enough. I played in some games and hardly ever had a touch."*
I will always remember Leeds because... One of his five kids was born on the day of his final game for Leeds against Spurs in 1980.
Other clubs: Too many to mention but he went to Bury on 3 different occasions.

A journeyman in the true meaning of the word: Exactly. He quit the game in 1990 at Hartlepool.
Then what? He trained to be a butcher but did not complete the course. During the lessons he noticed lorry loads of meat being delivered for them to practice on. He gave up any ambitions to be a butcher and went into the cold meat distribution game.
How interesting: Initially he started supplying hotels, butchers, cafes and bakeries and then got a good social services contract. That was good enough to have his name etched on to the side of his van.
So he owns the business? It's not massive (3 vans) but at least it's his own little empire. They're called *Wayne Entwhistle's Farm Fresh Foods* and it has been going since 1990.
I'll bet that has some early starts: Just 5am everyday. He had a farming background pre-football so it's not a problem.
What else? Wayne also has a DJ business called Detroit Promotions that has been making weddings go with a bang since 2002. He doesn't spin the tunes himself anymore because his image isn't right. He employs DJ Grove Mama and DJ Deluxe who set the tone.
Did he do requests? Someone asked him to play 'Livin' on a Prayer' by Bon Jovi and the CD stuck. You can book Wayne's World for £180 a night and he'll do anything from weddings to birthday parties. He works 2/3 nights a month.
Lives: Bury.

Chris Fairclough

Age: 41.
First name: Courtney.
Leeds seasons: 6, from 1989 to 1995.
Awards: Supporters' 'Player of the Year' 1990.
Games: 240 (23 goals).
Position: Central defender.
Other clubs: Nottingham Forest, Tottenham, Bolton, Notts County and York City.
Injury time: Chris left Bolton in 1998 for Notts County but injuries took their toll and he returned to Yorkshire in the early part of 1999, joining York City when Neil Thompson was in charge.

If he was injured why did York take him on? Good question. Chris managed to play a few games but struggled to get fit, as back and hamstring injuries prevented him stringing many games together.

I can see a retirement coming on: Terry Dolan took over from Thompson, but Chris knew his playing days were coming to an end in his late thirties.

And back to Nottingham? That's where he was from so after quitting York by mutual consent in March 2001, he trained with Notts County for six weeks and played in a reserve game, but the next day he felt the old injuries return and decided to hang up his boots.

Did he stay in football? Chris landed a part-time job coaching Nottingham Forest's Under-12s and when Paul Hart was promoted to manager, vacancies arose for full-time staff and Chris was handed the job of coaching the Under-17s. It's a job he finds satisfying and rewarding and he has learned a great deal about psychological and mental skills.

Does he go anywhere without Chris Whyte? They may have seemed like inseparable partners at Leeds but they parted company in 1995.

Lives: Outside Nottingham with wife Amanda, daughters Hannah, 16, and Daisy, 7, and son Jordan, 13. The missus runs a theatre workshop in her spare time and Hannah wants to be a proper thespian.

Neil Firm

Aka: DI Firm or Guv'nor.
Age: 47.
Leeds era: 1976-1982.
Games: 12.
Position: Centre-half.
Were Leeds vulnerable? Only when he was on the team sheet.
Other clubs: Oldham and Peterborough.
Retired: Achilles injury 1986.

And into lion taming? It was the pub trade that took his fancy. Neil and his wife became landlords of the *Three Horse Shoes* in a town called Diss, in Norfolk.
That's a bit of a trek from his home in Peterborough: He knew Norfolk and had seen an advert for pub tenants, hence the application. He ran it for just over a year until 1988.
Then what happened? He joined Norfolk police as a bobby.
Was he on the beat? Yes, pounding the streets of Thetford. His first arrest was a drunken female. He was PC Firm 1053.
Does he still have that number? No. In 1991 he moved into plain clothes as a Detective Sergeant in CID.
What did he CID on? He targeted all the major crime of Norfolk from Kings Lynn to Great Yarmouth. Burglary, armed robbery and murder. They have about 17,000 incidents a year so he was kept busy.
Wasn't that Tony Martin bloke from Norfolk? Yes and when it all kicked off in 1999 Neil was on the case.
Them lads wouldn't have been shot if they hadn't been committing a crime in the first place: That may be but Neil was responsible for putting Martin behind bars.
I can see a promotion on the horizon. 2005 sees Neil as a Detective Inspector, the same rank as Jack Regan from the Sweeney.
Does he wear a kipper tie and get 24-hours to solve a case? No but he is in charge of 35 men and covert operations.
Meaning? They try to nick the low-life before the crimes are committed. Some of his officers do go out with guns.
Scary: If Neil shot like he defended, we would be in trouble.
Likely to say: *"Norfolk is the safest place in the country."*

Brian Flynn

Age: 50.
Height: 5′ 3″ and a half plus a bit.
Leeds era: 1977-1982.
Position: Midfield.
Reality: He was a hustler with a big heart.
Games: 177 (11 goals).
Wales international caps: 66
Other clubs: Burnley (twice), Cardiff, Doncaster (twice), Bury, Limerick (coach) and Wrexham (player/manager).
Retired: 1993.
Did he carry on at Wrexham? Yes and did well considering he was handed a suspect team and no money. He actually survived as manager for over 10 years until 2001.

Was he pushed? Nobody pushes our man Flynn. He took on a bigger challenge as manager at Swansea. He was sacked in early 2004. He should have known it was a manager's graveyard.

Pity: Next, Brian was in the frame for the Wales job which eventually went to John Toshack. The Mighty Flynn is currently in charge of the Welsh youth squads.

Brian on kiddie management: *"It is hugely rewarding developing the cream of young Welsh talent. Brought up at Turf Moor where Burnley had a great tradition for producing their own players, I always tried to do the same as a manager."*

Looking to South Africa: Brian's long-term aim is to produce players who will help Wales qualify for the 2010 World Cup finals in South Africa.

Leeds hero: Flynny will always be a hero with Leeds fans for the goal he scored in the 86th minute at Old Trafford in February 1981 - the last time the Whites defeated Manchester United at the Theatre of Dreams.

Does he dine out on that goal? Brian uses it to impress players too young to remember him playing.

Burnley based? It's an ideal base for getting around the country. Brian goes to the Welsh FA's offices in Cardiff when needed, but most of his time is spent travelling round clubs talking to players and managers and watching matches.

Johnny Giles

Age: 65.
Appearance: Your favourite uncle.
Leeds era: 1963-1975.
Games: 515 (115 goals).
Shirt: Number 10.
Role: Central midfield and penalty taker.
Other clubs: Manchester United, West Brom (player/manager), Shamrock Rovers (player/manager), Philadelphia Fury, Vancouver Whitecaps (coach), West Brom (second spell as manager). He also managed the Republic of Ireland team in 1980.

Retired: 1977.
Does Johnny have a bus pass? He is eligible for one. It hardly seems possible that the man who, with Billy Bremner, formed arguably the greatest midfield partnership in British football is now a pensioner with a replacement hip and grandchildren.
How does he spend his days? He is still in demand by the media and does an Irish version of 'Match of the Day'. Count in some Champions League and international matches and newspaper and radio work.
How did he get into the media? Around the time of the 1986 World Cup, he was asked to do a bit of work for sources in Dublin and it took off from there. Johnny is rated by those in the know as one of the shrewdest football brains in the business.
Still busy: Johnny is still on the after-dinner circuit and even in 2005 can carry 'An Evening With Johnny Giles'.
Where is he based? Birmingham but loves returning to his hometown of Dublin - *"a real international city"*.
Does he see the other Revie boys? *"We don't see much of each other but we do keep in touch."* They meet up at Revie era dinners and golf days.
What happens at these events? Johnny sings a few songs (O' Danny Boy) and answers questions from fans. Please form an orderly queue since he is a big draw.
Family: Lives with wife Ann and has seven grandchildren. Catherine has four children, Michael has two and Christopher has one.

Arthur Graham

Age: 53.
Leeds era: 1977-1983.
Games: 260 (48 goals).
Appearance: The Bay City Rollers union representative.
Role: Winger. Arthur and Carl Harris would tease opposition full-backs. He'd turn them inside out and have them running in circles. Those were the days.
Scotland caps: 10.
Claim to fame: Scored a four minute hat-trick (against Birmingham 1978). Goals in the 65th, 67th and 69th minutes.
Other accolades: 1981 Leeds United table tennis champion.

Other clubs: Cambuslang Rangers, Aberdeen, Manchester United, Bradford City (player/coach) and Halifax Town (coach).
Retired: 1987.
Football in the blood: Arthur has had a job in football ever since leaving school. Signed from Aberdeen by Jimmy Armfield for £125,000, he stayed at Elland Road for six years before moving to Manchester United for £45,000.
Coaching school: He coached at Halifax Town in 1988 under the management of his big pal Jim McCalliog before Paul Hart set up Leeds United's School of Excellence and Arthur has been coaching part-time for the Academy ever since.
The school run: He also coaches in schools and runs a soccer coaching company called First Touch.
Happy days: Arthur loved his time at Leeds United even though they didn't win anything to go with the bevvy of medals from his time at Aberdeen.
Lives: Wetherby, which is handy for the Academy at Thorp Arch, and he's a keen Leeds fan.
Arthur on troublesome kids: *"I'm never comfortable when I coach in some schools and they talk about Man U 'scum'. I get on to them right away about that. Alan Smith would have been one of those kids who called Man U 'scum', yet he ended up going there."* You tell 'em Arthur.
Little Grahams: He has five children, including three in three years when he started a new family. The youngest is ten and he reckons they keep him young.

Eddie Gray MBE

Age: 57.

Leeds era (as player): 1963-1984.

Games: 572 (67 goals - including those two against Burnley in 1970).

Position: Left winger. In the days when dribbling got you into the first team not dropped from it.

Injury prone: From 1970-1975 Eddie only managed 82 league games.

A rare breed: Eddie played for just the one club. How's that for dedication. He was rightly awarded the MBE in 1983.

Retired (from playing): 1984.

Surely Leeds found him a job: He got the top job in 1982. He steered the club through bouts of mid-table obscurity during the Division 2 years. He lasted until 1985. Soon after, he went up to Middlesbrough as their reserve and youth team coach, then to Rochdale as manager, and to Hull City in 1988.

And back to Leeds? After a stint of unemployment Eddie returned as coach to George Graham in 1995, but was sacked as assistant manager in May 2003 after Peter Reid took over. The managerial yo-yo was back when he was appointed caretaker-manager on Reid's sacking in 2003, but was sacked again in May 2004 after failing to keep Leeds in the Premiership.

Keeping fit: Despite all the injuries, Eddie completed the 2005 London Marathon in a time of 4hrs 19mins. However, cramp struck at the 16 mile mark and a hamstring problem caused him to pull up after 20 miles, and he walked the remaining distance.

Was I dreaming or was Eddie wearing a Sunderland shirt? Eddie was persuaded to wear a Sunderland shirt by Black Cats chairman Bob Murray, who donated a four figure sum to charity.

I'll be back: Eddie has not discounted at being a football manager again. *"You can never say never. Forty-two years in the game is a long time and I really enjoyed it but I am also enjoying having a bit more time to take holidays and see more of the world."* The Gray's went to South Africa this summer.

Lives: With wife Linda at Kirkby Overblow near Harrogate.

Frank Gray

Age: 50
Leeds era: 1970-1979, and 1981-1985.
Games: 407 (35 goals).
Position: Left back or left midfield.
Scotland caps: 32.
Is he related to Eddie Gray? They're brothers. They also both scored on their full debuts and Eddie brought Frank back to the club when he was manager.
Retired: 1992.
Other clubs: Nottingham Forest, Sunderland, Darlington (player/manager), Blackburn (scout), Sheffield Wednesday

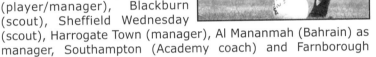

(scout), Harrogate Town (manager), Al Mananmah (Bahrain) as manager, Southampton (Academy coach) and Farnborough Town (manager).
New job: When Farnborough Town were relegated from the Nationwide Conference they appointed Frank as manager on May 5, 2005. He accepted a two-year contract.
Frank on Farnborough: *"I watched them in their last three games before agreeing to take the job, and hopefully I can put a smile back on the faces of the people who support Town."*
Middle East connections: Frank took charge of Al Mananmah in Bahrain in 1994, and can recommend the experience. His team was made up of part-timers but they had great natural ability. He says some of his players are not far off being World Cup material.
And back to the UK: Between returning from Bahrain and landing the Farnborough job, Frank coached at the Southampton Academy and scouted for Nottingham Forest. He also found time to indulge in one of his favourite hobbies, golf.
Home: Hayling Island. The place where the phantom beach hut arsonist is on the loose.
Family matters: Frank's son Andy followed in the footsteps of the Grays by joining Leeds. He's currently at Sheffield United.
European Cup medals: Frank had the honour of playing in two European Cup finals for different British clubs. He collected a winners medal with Forest in 1980 and a losers medal with Leeds five years earlier.

Brian Greenhoff

Age: 52.
Leeds era: 1979-1982.
Appearance: Young country and western singing sensation.
Games: 78 (1 goal – against. Nottingham Forest 1980).
Position: Full back or midfield.
Other clubs: Manchester United and Rochdale.
Retired: 1984.
The brothers: Brian had an older brother called Jimmy who also played for Leeds in the 1960s.
Was his stint at Leeds a good one? It filled a gap. Injuries, a personality clash with the then

manager Allan Clarke and a dispute with a member of the board over money made things difficult. He left in 1982.
The pub trade: Brian was brought up in a pub in Barnsley so it was natural that when he retired from football he should take a pub. He ran the *Hare and Hounds* in Rochdale, but with three young kids the job didn't work out and he wasn't happy.
Pity: After a year in the pub trade, he tried to get back into sport but got no replies from football clubs. He says he got the interviews but was always too outspoken.
Not like Brian Clough eh: He ended up running a plush snooker hall in the centre of Manchester. There were no fewer than 65 snooker tables with Hendry, Davis and Higgins among top names that would practice there. Six months after Brian left, the club closed because they couldn't fill it every night and it wasn't making enough money.
I guess he needs something more settled: That happened when he got a job in the early 1990s as a sports rep for William Lindop Ltd. He used to flog gear to shops along the M25 corridor.
Calling all ex-pats: In 2004 Brian and his wife Maureen moved from Rochdale to Menorca, where they have an apartment. He works for a restaurateur during the holiday season.
Keeping in touch: Like every house in Menorca, they have Sky TV to keep tabs on the English football. Even the toilets have Sky over there.

Peter Haddock

Age: 43.
Leeds era: 1986-1992.
Nickname: 'Fish'.
Position: Midfield or defence.
Accolades: Supporters Player of the Year in 1988.
Games: 144 (1 goal). 15,000 saw him score against Swindon in 1987.
Other clubs: Newcastle and Burnley (loan).
Retired: 1991 at Leeds.
Making some dough: 'Fish' and his wife Deborah ran a bakery for a while after injury forced him to retire from football aged 30.

Stand and deliver: Next he had a go at being a postman which was a godsend since it took him into his current job as a courier.
How did he get into that? By chance. His contacts at the Post Office made it possible for him to consider setting up on his own and it has worked. These days he's too busy to even take stage two of his coaching badge.
Does he still look out for Leeds' results? Being a Geordie you'd think Peter would be a member of the 'Toon Army' but his allegiance is still to Leeds. Sons Peter, 19, and Carl, 15 are big Leeds supporters.
Does he go to many games? Haddock senior watched the final home game of the 2004 season against Charlton.
Following in Shearer's footsteps: The young Haddocks have turned out for Cramlington Juniors - the boy's club Alan Shearer played for. So far there have been no approaches from Football League clubs so Peter Jnr is working for the DSS.
Memories: Versatile, 'Fish' always preferred playing in defence, though he also operated in midfield. He missed the whole of the Division 1 Championship season and the 1987 promotion play-offs, though he played a big part in United's Division 2 Championship season.
Lives: It's only natural that with his surname he should live by the sea. His converted barn overlooks the sea, high on a hill at Seaton Sluice, Northumberland. The wind often blows from the north so you need your thermals even inside the house.

Gunnar Halle

Age: 40.
Born: Oslo, Norway.
National record: Gunnar was Norway's 100 metre record holder for Under-12s.
Leeds era: 1996-1999.
Games: 86 (4 goals). It actually took Halle over 50 games before he scored his first goal. In his younger days Halle was a 60 goals a season man when he played as a striker. Even at Oldham he scored between 8 and 10 a season.
So why did he score so few at Leeds? Maybe it was because he was in the same side as

Jimmy Floyd Hasselbaink. Maybe it was his defensive role.
Key asset: His versatility.
O'Leary on Halle: *"I could not have a better squad player than Gunnar who can come and do a great job in any defensive position."*
Not first choice then? As the quote suggests, it was a squad game when O'Leary took over. Eight players for each position.
International caps: 64.
Other clubs: Larvik Gurn, Lillestrom, Oldham, Bradford City (of course), Wolverhampton on loan and Lillestrom again.
Retired: 2002. That's just English football. He went back to Norway to play for Lillestrom for a further season.
Coaching: In 2003 he became the club's youth team coach. At the start of the 2004/05 season he was promoted by manager Jan Aage Fjortoft as the first team coach which is where he is today. The team are currently mid-table.
Near miss experience: Gunnar nearly missed the boat when it came to playing for Leeds. After Oldham, the Leeds deal fell through when Howard Wilkinson was sacked in 1996. Gunnar was preparing to go back to Norway when the club had a change of heart and made him George Graham's first signing.
Last visit to Elland Road: May 2005 for the Lucas Radebe Testimonial.

Peter Hampton

Age: 50.
Leeds era: 1971 – 1980.
Position: Left Back.
Little known fact: Peter was on the bench for the 1975 European Cup Final and can still fit into the suits they had made for the occasion.
Did he play much? Not a lot considering he was at the club for 9 seasons. He played reserve football for the first five years.
Why? He had to wait for Terry Cooper to retire, Frank Gray to move into midfield and Trevor Cherry to leave the club.

Taking his opportunity: Once he was in, he played 76 times.
Other clubs: Stoke (1980-1984), Burnley (1984-1987), Rochdale then Carlisle (1987).
Retired: 1987. He then worked at Carlisle from 1988 for 11 years as physio, assistant manager, and coach. Peter and Mervyn Day, the manager, were sacked when Michael Knighton took control in 1999.
It's dog eat dog: Peter then picked up a job at Bury as physio until 2000 when he became manager of non-league team Workington Town, and the team won promotion to the UniBond League.
But? After 3 years he was sacked.
The Big Issue beckons: Actually Peter's in therapy. Physiotherapy. In 2002 he became a fully qualified Chartered Physiotherapist and has letters after his name. Peter Hampton BSC (Hons).
Sounds posh: He had a part-time surgery at a health club called Sands in Carlisle in 2003 but today does most of his work at Carlisle's School of Excellence. Currently, he also has time to sell leisure wear for a company called ISIS.
Isn't that like Lord Robert Winston having a car boot sale? ISIS employed him whilst he was doing his degree so he just kept with them because he liked the job.
What's his title? Sales Executive and Peter is their front man.
Lives: Carlisle with wife and two kids.
Golf: His playing partner is David McNiven.

Gary Hamson

Age: 46.
Leeds era: 1979-1986.
Games: 152 (4 goals).
Role: Midfield bull terrier.
Other clubs: Sheffield United, Bristol City and Port Vale.

Injury: In the final game of Allan Clarke's reign as manager (against West Brom) Hamson was already leaving the club. Frank Gray couldn't play so Hamson stepped in as a favour and badly injured his knee.
What happened to the move to the other club? The deal was off. What's more he'd sold his house in Leeds, his wife was expecting, they were living with parents and he was a cripple. Life never got so low.
Retired: 1988 at Port Vale (he left Leeds in 1986).
What does a retired player do? Gary went to sell assurance for a company called Refuge Assurance in Derby. He rose from an area rep to Sales Development Manager.
Sounds good: In 1999 when the company merged, Gary sued for unfair dismissal. They settled out of court.
So he wasn't welcomed back at the office? Hardly. He then spent 6 months working as a financial advisor for a company in Matlock before moving to York in 2000.
Why York? That's where the work was. In 2004 he set up his own business called Hallmark East Midlands Ltd selling financial advice. He has a degree in the subject so why not.
Also: He likes to get things done and was elected as a Liberal Democrat councillor for West Hallam in 2001. In 2002 he was promoted to the Borough Council of Erewash.
I like the Lib Dems: They have zero tolerance to litter.
So we have a future Prime Minister in our midst? In true political tradition the answer is 'yes' and 'no'. He thinks becoming an MP could dilute the work he can do on a local level but he likes a challenge and never had the number 10 as a player.
I like him: He's also the agent of Celtic's most promising youngster Aiden McGready.
Family: Married to Sandra, with four children and lives in West Hallam.

Ray Hankin

Age: 49.
Leeds era: 1976-1980.
Appearance: Russian debt collector.
Games: 103 (netted 36 times).
Not a bad goal tally: Most of these were scored with headers. When he had the ball at his feet he had the touch of an elephant.
Best sending off: Too many to mention.
Myths dispelled: Ray introduced slopping out on the Leeds bus which in those days did not have the luxury of having an on-board toilet.

Time for a sharp exit: Ray went to Canada to play for Vancouver Whitecaps. In 1982 he came back to the UK to play for Arsenal. That didn't work out and he was dispatched to Shamrock Rovers, then Vancouver again, and Middlesbrough in 1982. Peterborough and Wolves followed.
Retired: 1985. Ray did turn out for part-timers Whitby Town in 1986 and Blue Star and fully retired in 1987 playing for Guisborough.
What did he do for work other than part-time football? In 1986 Ray got a job in a mental hospital near Middlesbrough.
He restrained a few nutters whenever I saw him play: He still had that temper at the end of his playing career. Whilst at Peterborough he was sent off 5 times in one season and in his final game at Guisborough he also got a red card.
Maybe working at the hospital was a cry for help: It wasn't for long. In 1988 he became manager of Northallerton Town until 1991.
Today: Big Ray can be found working up at Newcastle United as the Football in the Community officer. He's been at it for some years.

Carl Harris

Age: 49.
Era: 1973-1982.
Position: Winger.
Speciality: Leaving defenders for dead. He was quick.
Goals: 29.
Previous Clubs: Briton Ferry.

That well-known Premier League side? Carl actually preferred playing against men rather than having an apprenticeship playing with boyos his own age.

It must have been a dream coming to Leeds? They were a major force in those days and Revie brought him in at the tender age of 16.

High point? Scoring on his debut against Ipswich after coming on to replace Johnny Giles. He ranks that alongside playing for Wales and being asked to train with the Leeds 1st team by Don Revie as a 16-year old.

A big talent: He never really fulfiled his true potential but was excellent value. He became fed up with the club's decline and revolving door management style. He saw out his contract and left of his own free will.

Retired: 1989 at Exeter City. He was living in South Wales and fed up with all the travelling, decided enough was enough.

What did he do? In 1990 he started working in his father-in-law's removal business. He still works there today so if you want a Steinway shifting then call Neath Port Talbot Removals. Cheap as chips but don't expect him to turn up sporting a moustache.

What happened to football management? He dabbled as player/manager of Briton Ferry from 1992-1994. After a string of bad results he brought in his van to remove himself from the manager's job.

So does he have a large fleet? No, just the single white van that he drives himself. It doesn't even have his name on the side. He likes the job and sometimes finishes at 1:30 in the afternoon.

To play golf? He doesn't play but does enough weight training to help him hump all day.

Family? He's married with 3 daughters.

Paul Hart

Age: 52.
No relation to: Ian Harte.
Appearance: A Greek God.
Games: 191 (16 goals).
Strengths: Tackling, heading.
Weaknesses: His flaws were rarely exposed.
Tony Currie says: *"He was undoubtedly one of the best defenders never to be capped by England."*
Roommate: Trevor Cherry away, Brian Flynn at home.
Eh? For home games, commuters Paul and Brian would stay over at the Dragonara Hotel on the eve of matches.

Leeds high point? League Cup semi-final against Southampton.
Low point? Relegation in 1982.
After Leeds: Notts Forest, Sheffield Wed, Birmingham and Notts County.
Retired: 1988. He immediately took on the manager's job at Chesterfield.
I'll bet that was a real rollercoaster ride: Paul left after an unremarkable one season in charge to look after youth set-ups at Forest then Leeds alongside Eddie Gray.
Didn't he do well: Paul was a major factor in Leeds winning the FA Youth Cup in 1993 and 1997. He went back to Forest in 1999 after he told George Graham he had taken the youngsters as far as he could. David Platt left Forest and Hart was promoted to manager in 2001.
He was touted as the next Leeds manager in 2004: He was but decided to stay at Forest. He'd done well in the previous season but was sacked when they started badly to the 2004/05 campaign. Look at them now!
Was he out of work for long? A month. With his excellent potential, Barnsley took him as manager even though Paul had to drop a division. After less than six months in charge things were not working out. In the Spring of 2005, Paul left the club by mutual consent.
Strange but true: There is another Paul Hart trying to contact every other Paul Harts in the world.

David Harvey

Age: 57.
Position: Goalkeeper.
Appearance: A pin-up for *Planet of the Apes* fans.
Nickname: Suave.
Era: 1965-1985 (with an interim spell in Canada for 3 years).
Disappointing: Harvey missed the European Cup Final in 1975 through injury.
Games: 446. He did have the opportunity to score but missed the only penalty he took.
Brought back: By Eddie Gray in 1982 and made captain. It was Lorimer, Gray and Harvey all playing to a half-empty Elland Road.

After Leeds: Bradford City, Partick Thistle and Morton.
Retired: 1986.
I'd heard he liked farming? For much of his time at Leeds he had a 100-acre place out near Driffield. He used the land to farm beef cattle. He was often down the market and abattoir when he should have been training.
Nice: Harvey also ran a pub called *The Swordsman* near York and bred dogs, which was his hobby.
What type of dogs? Poodles and West Highland Terriers.
When did he move to the Orkney's? You have done your homework. He sold up in Yorkshire and went there in 1993. He bought himself a lovely 15-acre plot to tend cattle and breed dogs. He's been there ever since.
Is it a tightknit community? All the crofters know each other and there are only two pubs on the island. He's also the local postman.
So he delivers letters and dogs? When this interview was being conducted we had to cut it short because one of his bitches was having pups.
Did he name any after former Leeds players? *"I would name one after Norman Hunter but Norman would only kick, not bite."*
Harvey on the weather: *"It's better than it is down in Yorkshire."*

John Hawley

Aka: Lovejoy.
Age: We might have to use carbon dating.
Why's that? Well, he's an antique dealer.
You mean Brian Deane's agent? No proper antiques. Fine art, furniture, china, that type of thing.
Where does Leeds United fit into all this? John played for the club for a single season in 1978. Despite being the top scorer he was sold to Sunderland in 1979.
Bad decision? Ask Jimmy Adamson.

Other clubs: Arsenal, Leyton Orient, Hull, Bradford and finally Scunthorpe.
Retired: 1986.
That's when he trained to be an antique dealer? You don't train, you have it in your blood and John was born into it with his dad, Ray, having an antiques shop for over 40 years. Hawley didn't turn pro (with Hull) until he was 21 because he was busy working in the business.
So he always kept his hand in? Since retiring, John built up the antiques side of things and they have a shop near Beverley. In 2002 he launched an auctioneering business called Hawley's Auctioneers, Valuers and Agents...they once sold a painting for £52,000.
That's more than Seth gets a week! Could he give a value on the current Leeds side? Shall we start the bidding at £1?
Does he say 'cheap as chips'? No. It takes him about two months to get the antiques together but he does the selling himself. Going once, going twice and all that.
Would we recognise him today? You could under all the upholstery. He normally has stubble.
He won't have time to run a boozer? No but he co-runs a B&B called *The Albion* with his partner, Caroline. They also own a couple of properties in France which they rent out, and he's an agent to a couple of lower league footballers.
If that isn't enough: He has three kids and a website to run.
Hates: Minimalism.

John Hendrie

Age: 42.
Born: Lanarkshire.
Middle name: Grattan.
Known for: Skill, speed and having the hairiest legs in football.
Leeds era: 1989-1990.
Games: 31 (5 goals).
Position: Winger.
Eye-to-eye: He didn't see it with Howard Wilkinson. He was sold to Middlesbrough and played injury free for six seasons, scoring 19 Premier League goals in the 1993/94 season.

Other clubs: Coventry, Hereford United (loan), Bradford City, Newcastle United and Barnsley.
Retired: 1999. In the same season he took over as manager of Barnsley. It lasted just 9 months but if you ever need a lawyer...
Why? What has he done? The former 'wizard of the wing', known to Bradford City fans as 'Skin 'em Johnny', is now a sports consultant with the Bradford based solicitors *Last Cawthra Feather.*
Does he don a gown and wig? Not on your life. John's a go-between, forming a link between lawyers and clients. Although sports contracts are his specialty, John can also arrange house conveyances and wills. Everyone needs legal work and some players prefer using lawyers to agents.
Any footballing links? John has his own show on Middlesbrough Football Club's TV station and has covered his old club in Europe. He also works as an expert summariser on BBC Radio Leeds, covering Bradford City where he and Stuart McCall became Valley Parade legends.
Not much scope for other interests then? John enjoys his golf but with four Hendries all under 18 there's not a lot of time. John and his wife Linda live at Menston.
Good memories of Leeds? He spent just one season there, but winning promotion with Howard Wilkinson's team in 1990 was special. John had a bad time with injuries at Elland Road, unlike his spell at Bradford where he missed only one of their 130 league games.

Vince Hilaire

Age: 46.
Lives: London.
Nickname: 'Vince the Prince'.
Position: Right-winger.
Games: 50 (7 goals).
Era: Bremner to Wilkinson.
Strengths: Dribbling.
Weaknesses: Getting stuck in – he was only 5' 6".
Other clubs: Crystal Palace, Luton Town, Portsmouth, Stoke and Exeter.
Retired: 1992.
And into non-league action: In 1993 Vince spent two seasons as co-manager and occasional player for Havant & Waterlooville in the 'we use ageing ex-pros' league.

It was said Vince didn't have a ruthless streak as a player, never mind a manager: The manager duties were split 50/50 (like good cop, bad cop). Along with ex-Palace team-mate Billy Gilbert, they did okay in their first season but then struggled. It became clear that co-managing a team wasn't an ideal way to run a club so he left in 1995. He immediately started working as a hospitality host at Palace on match days.

Not bad. Working just eighteen days a year? That's not the full story. From 1996-2002 he became honorary president of a football coaching school in Portsmouth called *Soccer World*.

So we'll soon have loads of Vince clones on the scene: If they have half the skill he had then football would be greatly enhanced.

What does he teach them? Dribbling, tricks, keepy-uppy, catching the ball in the back of the neck.

What else is he doing these days? Vince kept his Portsmouth connections and still lives in the area. He does some Pompey-punditry work for Quay Radio and works as a match day host at the club.

Leeds high point? Signing for the club was great and Vince reckons John Sheridan was one of the best players he ever saw.

Hobbies: Watching films – his favourite is *'White Heat'* with Jimmy Cagney.

Pop idol? *The Beloved* think so. They used his name in their 1990 hit song *'Hello'*.

Kevin Hird

Age: 53.
Born: Colne.
Leeds era: 1979-1984.
Aka: Jasper (because he resembles Jasper Carrott). They call him Jasper to this day, but Kevin reckons the real Jasper can't play the guitar as well as him!
Why's that? Kevin has a keen interest in music and guitar is his favourite instrument. He used to play in a band called *Visage*.
Games: 200 (21 goals).
That's not a bad return: Managers didn't know where to

play him since he could shoot, dribble, tackle and overlap so he was often played further up the field than in the full-back position he was bought for. He also took the penalties.
How much was he bought for? A British record fee for a full-back when Leeds signed him from Blackburn for £357,000.
Other clubs: Blackburn Rovers and Burnley.
Retired from pro football: 1986. He did prolong his playing days with some amateur clubs in and around Colne though.
Main job now? Support Assistant to a special needs school in Colne. The kids range from toddlers up to 16 and Kevin draws immense satisfaction from seeing them develop their talents.
Other jobs: Coaching at Blackburn Rovers' Centre of Excellence for the last six years. Damien Duff was one of his pupils to make the big time. Before that, Kevin ran his own coaching school for ten years in the East Lancashire, Skipton and Keighley areas. He also worked in a timber merchants.
Any other strings to his bow? Painting in watercolours. 'Jasper' is a good enough artist to sell his landscape pictures.
Family: Married with three grown up children. Jennifer, 23, was born while Kevin was a player at Leeds. Sam, 21, is a musician and attends Manchester University, while Jessica, 18, has won a place at York University.

Steve Hodge

Born: Nottingham.
Age: 42.
Leeds era: 1991-1994.
Games: 66 (10 goals).
Position: Midfield.
That's not a bad hit rate from midfield: You always felt you had a chance with Steve on the pitch although he was past his best when he came.
Other clubs: Nottingham Forest (twice), Aston Villa, Tottenham, Derby (loan), QPR, Watford. Academy coach at Forest, Leicester and Notts County.
Retired: 1998.

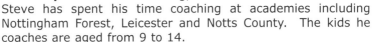

Academy coach: After retiring, Steve has spent his time coaching at academies including Nottingham Forest, Leicester and Notts County. The kids he coaches are aged from 9 to 14.
Is he another ex-footballer into a media job? Yes. You get paid for the only thing you can talk about. He spent a year working for Talk Radio in London and when that finished he went on a coaching course at Lilleshall with the likes of Steve Bould and Tony Adams. Hodgey hopes to get his UEFA coaching license and is looking to use the qualification in a coaching or managerial capacity. He needn't worry about management turning his hair grey. The grey hairs have already sprouted.
Mexico 1986: Steve was instrumental in one of the most talked about events in England's football history. He ballooned the ball into the path of Maradona's hand in that fateful match against Argentina in the World Cup.
Rumour has it: Hodgey was given Maradonna's shirt at full time. It's locked away but on show in a glass case at the National Football museum.
Steve the crusader: Currently Steve is leading a player's petition for Brian Clough to be knighted.
Lives: Near East Midlands Airport and enjoys watching football. He keeps in touch with former Leeds players Chris Fairclough and John Pemberton who coach at the Forest Academy.
Debut: Steve had the satisfaction of scoring on his debut for Leeds against Sheffield Wednesday.
Family: Steve has a son, a stepson and a daughter.

Norman Hunter

Age: 62.
Nickname? Norman 'Bites Yer Legs'.
Did he really 'bite legs'? Even Steve 'you beaut' Irwin would not have gone near him.
Games: 724 (21 goals).
Reputation: He was one of the hardest tacklers in the game.
International caps: 28.
Shirt number: 6.
Strengths: A supreme all-round defender.
Era: 1962-1976.
After Leeds: Bristol City and Barnsley.
Retired: 1983.

Did Norman, like most of his Revie team-mates, take up management? He did and it was Barnsley who signed Norman in 1980. He managed the side until 1984. After that he had a go down the road at Rotherham from 1985-1987.
But the magic wasn't there: His heart was at Leeds but he did the best he could.
I bet his defenders knew how to tackle: His method wasn't exactly PC. Today he would get sent off in every game.
What did Norman do after management? He had sports shops in Headingley and Bristol. They used to specialise in shin-pads. He didn't work in them himself but would pop in occasionally to test out the football boots on the manager. He also had a brief stint at selling life insurance.
Just what the players needed when he was on the pitch: In the late 1980s he got into the normal stuff you would associate with a Leeds legend: he coached kids and hit the after-dinner circuit.
What's he doing these days? Since 1993 he's been a regular Leeds match co-commentator on BBC Radio Leeds. He has also published his biography called 'Biting Talk'.
He's undoubtedly still a massive Leeds fan: He really enjoys the involvement with the club and supporters, and can often be seen around Leeds either playing golf or doing his after-dinners.
Likes: Spanish villa holidays.
How has he aged? 8 out of 10.

Denis Irwin

Age: 40.
Born: Cork.
That means he must have played for the Republic of Ireland? Only the 56 times and in two World Cups.
Leeds era: 1982-1986. Leeds was his first club.
Another Eddie Gray signing: He was an astute manager was Eddie and the fact that Irwin made the most of his career away from Elland Road, even winning a European Champions League winners medal, suggests it was a mistake to let him go.

Games: 80 (1 goal - against Notts County in 1985).
Debut: Against Scunthorpe in the FA Cup defeat in 1984.
Other clubs: Oldham, Manchester United and Wolves.
Retired: 2004. In his final game for Wolves, Denis was taken off in the 89th minute so he could receive the individual applause of the crowd. Nice touch.
No regrets: Wolves did keep the offer of another season open to Denis but he knew it was time to call it a day. He's now hoping to get a job in football as a coach. Denis has been taking his coaching badges but as yet no firm offers have come in from clubs willing to take him on. He is happy to get all the qualifications under his belt before dipping his toe into the coaching waters and Wolves (the club he supported as a boy) would be his first choice.
Leeds should take him back: In 1992 they tried to. Howard Wilkinson made the initial enquiry to Manchester United but it all turned sour when not only did Denis stay at Old Trafford but he was joined by Eric Cantona.
Lives: Manchester with his wife and kids.
Irwin on retirement: *"It is difficult to prepare for it. It is like falling off the end of a cliff. One second, something is there, and the next it's not. Football is your life for 22 years and then it is just gone."*
Hobbies: Tennis, golf and snooker.

Richard Jobson

Age: 42.
Didn't he play with The Skids? In some games yes but he's not the musical bloke.
Leeds era: 1995-1998.
Games: 26 (1 goal – an equaliser against Wimbledon in a 1-1 draw at Elland Road in December, 1995).
Sick note: Richard was sidelined for much of his spell at Elland Road where, along with David Wetherall, he became the club's PFA representative, a role that was to help qualify him for his present job as General Executive at the PFA in Manchester.

Other clubs: Watford, Hull, Oldham, Southend (on loan), Man. City, Tranmere, and Rochdale.
Retired: 2003 (aged 40).
Bright lad: Richard played for England Universities, studying Civil Engineering at Nottingham University, only to cut his studies short when Watford signed him in November, 1982.
When did he join the PFA? Just three months after finishing his playing career at Rochdale, Richard had a job waiting for him with the Players' Union where he has worked for 18 months.
Isn't that the organisation where Gordon Taylor is forever the chief executive? Yes but Jobson was not far behind, eventually becoming chairman in 2002 (a 12-month contract).
How many footballers does he represent? The PFA has around 4,000 current players on its books and nearly 50,000 former players. Part of Richard's job is to assess Premiership refs.
Easy. They're rubbish: He advises players over discipline and disputes. He was at Leeds on official business for Leeds' 2004 pay freeze debacle. He also assesses medical costs for players, and sources education courses for past and present players. Richard is a trustee of two PFA pension schemes.
What about those awards? The Oscars of the soccer world – the PFA's Player of the Year. Even though he's still a fan of the club he can't sway the judges to award it to a Leeds player.
Family life: Wife Sue and three kids.

Matthew Jones

Born: Llanelli.
Age: 24.
Leeds era: 1993-2000.
Games: 33 (no goals).
Other club: Leicester.
Position: Midfield.
Wales caps: 13.
Retired: 2004.

That's early: Matthew was only 23 when injury forced him to hang up his boots.
What type of injury? Knees and back.
Matthew on his bad back: *"I've had every possible treatment and even went as far as having surgery which had a risk of paralysing me from the waist down."*
The game isn't that important: He should have seen it coming. When he left Leeds in 2000 he signed for Leicester but hardly played a game after 2002 when the injuries became too much.
Final game: That was for Wales against the USA in May 2003. They lost 2-0 but it was his 13th cap and he was red carded so it was not the best game on which to finish your career and another victory for the superstitious society.
Discovery channel: When Matthew won the FA Youth Cup with Leeds in 1993 he was rated one of the most outstanding Welsh prospects the club had produced. He was found by former Leeds keeper Glan Letheran and joined the club at 12. Considering we signed him as a schoolboy and later sold him for £3.25 million, he was good business for Leeds.
Did he have any injuries at Leeds? Not as such, but he did contract meningitis in 2000. He was diagnosed between the UEFA Cup matches against Roma and Slavia Prague and was feeling wobbly on the bench for the home game against Prague.
So what is happening these days for Matthew? He has been doing radio and TV work – his good looks and expert opinions make him a natural for TV and we are likely to see much more of him on our screens in the future. Maybe he'll follow in the footsteps of Lee Sharpe on Celebrity Love Island. Matthew used to clean Lee's boots at Leeds so the 'Sharpster' owes him one.

Mick Jones

Age: 60.
Era: 1967-1975.
Appearance: Elder statesman of the Mormon Church.
Position: Centre-forward.
Previous club: Sheffield United (1962-1967).
Games: 312 (111 goals).
Retired: Due to injury in 1975.
High point: 1972 FA Cup Final. He dislocated his shoulder and was helped up by Norman Hunter to receive his medal from the Queen.

And so to work... Mick became a sales rep in 1975 for a sports leisure wear company called *Sondico*.

His patch was? The Northeast, even though he was still based in Leeds. He was selling tracksuits and football kits but eventually had enough of all the travelling and packed it in.

To do what? He opened 'Mick Jones Sports' in Maltby in 1982. It was a small shop selling all sorts of sporting goods.

Did he sell slings like the one he wore in the cup final? Did they come in small, medium and large? I don't think Mick sold them even though he told us that if he had the sling today he would be selling it on eBay for a fortune.

You mean to say he didn't keep it along with his sock tags? Afraid not. He doesn't know what happened to it.

How long did the shop last? 15 years until one day, out of the blue, somebody came in and bought it from him for his son to run.

Did it make him a fortune? No, although his own son had just been made redundant and so together they set up a market stall selling sports clothing. Together they travelled the markets of South Yorkshire for 2 years.

Currently: In 2000 Mick gave up the market stall when his son got a new job. Mick now does corporate work for Leeds.

Going back to that dislocated arm; does it give him any gyp? It certainly does. He has arthritis in it and it affects his golf swing.

What else? He had a book out in 2002 called '*Life & Times*', and likes walking in his spare time.

Vinnie Jones

Age: 40.
Former trade: Hod carrier.
Leeds era: 1989-1990.
Games: 44 (2 goals).
Other clubs: Wimbledon, Sheffield United, Chelsea, Wimbledon and QPR.
Medals: Division 2 Championship winners 1990.
Retired: 1999.
Hadn't he already made a film by then? Lock, Stock & Two Smoking Barrels was his turbo charged launch site into super stardom. It was his first film so the most crucial.
How did he get the part? Guy

Ritchie met Vinnie via a mutual friend. Guy was casting for his first film and was looking for a hard man to play the part of Big Chris. It was a risk but it achieved all the publicity the film and Vinnie needed. Basically Vinnie played himself.
What followed? Madonna, John Travolta, Nicholas Cage, Brad Pitt. Vinnie mixes with 'A' list celebs.
So he won't be doing a remake of *On the Buses* with Reg Varney? Vinnie is a luvvie. He talks a good game on and off the film set. He even rents a place in Beverley Hills in the next canyon to Rod Stewart.
Has he made it? Spending £2500 on a pair of cuff links? What do you think? He also drives a Ferrari.
Awards: 'Best Actor' as voted by *Empire* film magazine.
Tats: Five including a Leeds badge on his left leg costing £60.
Other stuff: Too much to mention but he had a column in The Sun for six years; has appeared in ads, books, TV, stage shows, more adverts, more TV, makeover shows, biography, This Is Your Life...and he was the face of Bacardi Rum for five years.
Vinnie on acting: *"I don't want to be seen as the hard-man of cinema, I'd like to be more of an action man, like Bruce Willis."*
Vinnie on management: *"The only thing that would tempt me back into football at this stage is the Leeds job."*
Currently: Working on a film in West London called 'Action Star' but rumoured to be going back to Hollywood for X-Men 3.
Hobbies: Fishing, greyhound racing, shooting and hitting neighbours.

Joe Jordan

Age: 53.
Leeds era: 1970-1978.
Games: 221 (48 goals).
Position: Striker.
Role: To put the frighteners on opposition defences. On the pitch he was busier than his dentist.
Trademark goal celebration: One-armed salute (on the run) with mouth wide open.
So when did Joe's teeth actually leave Joe's mouth? It was early in his Leeds career in a reserve match against Coventry. He always left them out to make himself look meaner.

Other clubs: Morton, Manchester United, AC Milan, Verona, Southampton, Bristol City (player/manager), Hearts (manager), Celtic (assistant manager), Stoke (manager), Huddersfield Town (assistant manager), Portsmouth (coach).
Scotland caps: 52. He scored in 3 consecutive World Cups (1974, 1978, 1982)
Let's not forget Joe played for the mighty AC Milan: Don't remind him, what with Liverpool winning the 2005 Champions League Final. Joe was on holiday in Italy and sat in silence as events unfolded on TV in a bar packed with AC Milan fans.
Jordan on that game: *"It was just unbelievable. Nobody could have written the script. Milan were the better team but it was a fantastic achievement by Liverpool to hit back like that."*
Currently: Joe lives in Bristol but rents a place on the south coast where he is Portsmouth's first team coach. When he was between footballing jobs he worked for Sky and Channel Four, covering Italian football and the Champions League.
Does he look out for Leeds' results? He has taken a keen interest in Leeds and with their strong fan base, thinks they will climb back to the Promised Land.
Family: Joe and his wife Judith have four grown up children - two girls and two boys. Thomas, aged 24, plays centre back for Havant where former Leeds striker Ian Baird is the manager.
Current appearance: Thin and gaunt – a man with Premiership worries on his shoulders.

Chris Kamara

Born: Christmas Day, 1957.
Age: 48.
TV age: 9.
Leeds era: 1990-1991.
Appearance: Door-to-door jewellery salesman.
Specialty: The barnet and tache combo.
Games: 24 (1 goal).
Other clubs: Portsmouth, Swindon, Brentford, Stoke, Luton, Sheffield United and Middlesbrough.
Retired: 1995.
Then what? Did he get a job opening supermarkets as Lionel Ritchie? He became

manager of Bradford City (1995-1998) and then Stoke City (1998).

Media star: Chris has arguably become a bigger name in the media than he was as a footballer.

Present job: A Sky presenter, commentator and analyst. Chris has been on contract with Sky for five years and has resisted all attempts to prise him back into football management.

Surely somebody wants him? He was offered his old job at Bradford and admits to thinking long and hard at the time. Gillingham also wanted him and he spoke to their chairman before advising him on the appointment of Stan Ternent.

What if a job with a Premiership club comes up? He wouldn't leave Sky lightly. Football can be very insecure. Chris lasted 12 weeks as Stoke manager in 1998, before resigning because the club had long since developed a losing mentality that was difficult to shake off. He'd have left two weeks earlier if the chief executive hadn't been on holiday!

Jack-of-All-Trades: Chris is the only Sky Sports employee who combines presenting a Sunday morning show with commentating on the Coca Cola Championship and Carling Cup as well as reporting for the Soccer Saturday programme. He also has a column in the Sun newspaper.

Hobbies? Running. He did the London Marathon in 1999.

Family: Wife and two sons. They live near Wakefield.

Holidays: The family usually manage to get away to Tenerife where they have a villa.

Dylan Kerr

Age: 38.
Born: Malta.
Aka: 'The Legend' (a name given to him by Vinnie Jones)
At Leeds: 1989-1993.
Games: 20.
Position: Full back.
Other clubs: 14 in all.
Retired: 2003 at Hamilton Academicals.

Then what? Dylan got a job at Kilmarnock on the youth development programme. It was a part-time post and allowed him time to take his grown-ups coaching badge. On the course he met an American who ran a coaching school in Arizona. He was so impressed with Dylan's attitude and knowledge that he offered him a job at the school.

Called? West Valley United Soccer School. It was based at Glendale and Dylan was a big success with the pupils, so much so the director of coaching offered him a 3-year contract.

That's a long way from Hamilton Accies: One snag. After one year, he had to return to the UK to get his visa. His application is in but he is still awaiting the permit.

So what is he doing in the meantime? In 2004 Dylan gave it 6-months as a relief social worker for all the under age naughty boys in Paisley. He also did corporate work for Kilmarnock FC and has been the MC on match days.

Does he gee up the crowd like Delia Smith? And some. Dylan's a right character, the type of person you would want in your golfing 4-ball. Dylan is also popular as a DJ and tours the pubs and clubs of Troon with his CDs. If you go to *McIntyre's*, *The Loft* or *Pebbles* you'll see him.

What about keeping his hand in on the coaching front? The America job is pending but he has done stints with Colchester, Notts County and Kilwinning Rangers, helping them out as coach.

Last time in Leeds: 1995. He says he's still friendly with Gary Kelly.

Accent: If the film 'Kes' ever gets made into a Hollywood animated blockbuster then Dylan would get the voice-over job of Billy Casper. He's broad South Yorkshire.

David Kerslake

Age: 39.
Not to be confused with: Roundhay Park Lake
Games: 8.
Leeds era: Not so much an era more a mid-term break. Weather fronts stay for longer. For you statisticians out there it was 1993.
Position: Right-back.
What went wrong? Gary Kelly appeared on the scene.
Weaknesses: Injury.
Today's eBay value: £51.99 (including P&P).
Other clubs: Tottenham Hotspur, Swindon Town, Ipswich  Town, Wycombe Wanderers and Swindon Town again.
What Ipswich said about Kerslake: *"David arrived at Ipswich on a free and I think we paid too much for him."*
Retired from playing? In 1999 at Swindon due to injury.
Then what? Having gained his professional coaching badge David went back to White Hart Lane as Spurs' Academy Team Coach.
What's he up to nowadays? After Tottenham he joined Northampton Town in 2000 as Reserve Team Manager when old team-mate Colin Calderwood offered him the job.
How has it gone? A load of Cobblers? It's been a rollercoaster ride but they're doing okay. In fact David's quietly confident good times are not too far away. They have a fit, strong squad with some promising youngsters waiting in the wings or is that 'on the wings'?
Hobbies: Golf during his playing days. He doesn't get much chance these days.
High point at Leeds? He enjoyed working with Gary McAllister and Gordon Strachan. David still looks up to Strachan with all his coaching and tactical expertise.
Low point at Leeds: He ruptured his calf muscle against Liverpool at Anfield and never really recovered in his remaining time at Elland Road.

Gypsy Rose Lee

Era: 1971.
Born: 1372, Russia.
Appearances: 1.
Signed from: Blackpool Pier.
Objective: To lift the curse from Elland Road.
What curse? The curse that robbed Leeds of true domestic and European greatness.
Who'd believe that crap? The Don did. Revie thought the side's misfortune was down to the fact that Elland Road was built on the site of an ancient and sacred burial ground.
Did she line up with Bremner, Giles and Clarke?
She never even got on the bench. It was in the days before Sky so she would watch the matches on her crystal ball a few hours before kick off.
What about the curse? Leeds went on to win the FA Cup, and a league championship but still had some incredible bad luck.
Some clubs never won anything so you can hardly call Leeds unlucky: Wait until you hear this: They missed out on the double at Wolves. They were robbed of the European Cup, banned from Europe. And signed Peter Barnes.
That is bad: The curse must have been omnipresent too, since it travelled to away fixtures on the team bus.
They could have bought a new bus or gone on the train: They had no money in those days. All the spare cash went on sock tabs and camel hair coats.
Did she ever work in the game again? Doncaster, Hull and Carlisle all had reason to call her in.
With any success? What do you think?
After football: Gypsy Rose Lee went back to reading palms. Her booth burnt down due to unforeseen circumstances but as luck would have it she made a few quid selling ideas to ITV. Her look was adopted by Guns n' Roses and she became the Romany spokesperson on Radio 5. She now lives in Ireland where she organises caravan holidays.
Hobbies: Tarmac.
Busiest time of the week: 5pm Friday when the council offices have closed for the weekend.

Glan Letheran

Lovely name: It's 100% Welsh.
Age: 49.
Born: Llanelli, South Wales.
Leeds era: 1973-1977.
Position: Goalkeeper.
He must have been good because we were the best in those days: Well he only played twice but the fact he is still in the game today suggests he was a good understudy when Don Revie brought him to the club.
Debut: Against Hibernian in a UEFA Cup tie that went to penalties. His only other game was in the league against Ipswich.

Not a lot of people know this: Glan was on the bench in the 1975 European Cup Final.
Other clubs: Scunthorpe, Chesterfield and Swansea.
Retired: 1980. He did play on for a few clubs in non-league football but that was strictly part-time. His final game was for Bangor City in 1985.
Do keepers hang up their gloves or boots? Both. Glan moved back to Llanelli and became a carpet cleaner until he got into goalkeeping coaching at Swansea City under John Hollins. Since then he's been goalie coach at Exeter, Leicester, and Chester and is currently the Welsh scout for Southampton.
How many games does he watch? In a good week, four. Actually his scouting pedigree comes from 6 years he had at Leeds as Welsh scout from 1992-1998. He was responsible for bringing Matthew Jones to the club.
What was he doing when you spoke to him? He was in a hotel lobby in the middle of doing his final Pro License examinations. He's now as educated in that department as you can possibly be. He handles the media like he did crosses.
Does he come to Leeds much? Lots. His wife is from Rothwell.
Glan talking balls: *"Balls have changed so much since I was in goal so it is understandable you see keepers making huge cock-ups. Because it is so light, it can move in the air 3 ways and up to 3-4 yards. I teach all keepers to parry not catch."*

Andy Linighan

Born: Hartlepool.
Age: 43.
Leeds era: 1984-1986.
Games: 74 (4 goals).
Position: Centre half.
Money well spent: Credit goes to Eddie Gray. As a manager he could spot a good player. Even though Bremner got rid of him, Linighan went on to command a £1.3 million fee when he went to Arsenal. Leeds bought him for £20,000.
Other clubs: Hartlepool, Oldham, Norwich, Arsenal, Crystal Palace and Oxford United.
Retired: 2001.

Need a plumber? When 6ft 4in Andy retired he took a year out and then started a plumbing business in Harpenden. After leaving school at 16 he began a four-year apprenticeship in his home town of Hartlepool. He was in Hartlepool's first team at 18 but is glad now that he completed the final two years of his plumbing apprenticeship at 20.

Can he a fix my leaking tap? Of course but what spare time he has is spent doing country pursuits and he has been shooting several times with Vinnie Jones. Mind you, his plumbing business and family life take up most of his time. He and wife Wendy have five children: Kirsty, 19, Rachel, 17, Jessica, 13, James, 10, and Hannah Rose, 5.

He's obviously got a leak of his own. What memories does he have? Arsenal's FA Cup Final triumph over Manchester United on a penalty shoot-out brought back happy memories for Andy who scored the winning goal for the Gunners against Sheffield Wednesday in extra time in 1993. He watched the 2005 Final on TV and 'knew' Arsenal would win the penalty shoot-out.

So football is just a spectator sport these days? Andy has never fancied coaching and he reckons there are already too many ex-footballers on TV telling everybody how the game should be played! He's happy sticking to his plumbing.

Footballing family: Andy's twin brothers, Brian and John, played for Sheffield Wednesday and the other brother David for Ipswich, Blackpool and Dunfermline.

Peter Lorimer

Age: 59.
Aka: 'Hot-shot', 'The Lash'.
We all know who Peter Lorimer is, but could he actually kick the ball to 90 miles per hour? That was a myth. He was scientifically tested in the mid-70s and it came in at 76.5 miles per hour but he was the hardest kicker of his time.
Debut: Aged 15 and 289 days.
Goals: A record 238 in 701 matches. He would have the appearance record too but for a gap period from 1980-1984.
Other clubs: Toronto Blizzards, York City, Vancouver White Caps, and Cape Town City.

Retired: 1986. He went on to coach Haifa FC in Israel.
Did he convert to Judaism? Contrary to common belief he did not change his name to Alon Ben Avraham. Nor was he surgically pruned.
He did get the chop from his job? He merely returned to Leeds to pursue a career in public licensing.
How did he get into that game? One of the Leeds directors owned a sports and leisure club called *The Trafalgar* in Hunslet. Peter was offered the chance to run the operation.
I remember the gentlemen's evenings very well. Is it still there? The land is now a McDonald's. In 1990, the club was served a compulsory purchase order and knocked down.
Then what? Around the same time a friend, Graham Kane, was selling *The Commercial* pub, also in Hunslet, so Peter met with the brewery and took it over. He's still there.
Surely not serving? He still pulls the pints (£1.95) but prefers wine and whisky himself. When you speak to him he will break off to serve a lasagne. He's also a director at Leeds.
Good: His day starts at 6am and beer deliveries are Tuesdays.
What about radio? He used to have his own show on Radio Leeds in 2002 and did some commentating, but now he has official Leeds United duties at board level.
Books: In 1983 he wrote his own book called 'The Lash' and had a biography done on him in 2002.

John Lukic

Born: Chesterfield.
Real name: Jovan Lukic.
Age: 45.
Leeds era take 1: 1978-1983.
Leeds era take 2: 1990- 1996.
Games: 355.
Other club: Arsenal.
What's occurring today? Since leaving Arsenal in 2000, John has, in his own words, taken time out and done nothing.

Green fingered: The hands that saved countless shots during his two spells with Leeds and Arsenal are put to good use nowadays as green-fingered

John potters about in the garden. It gives him plenty of time for thought and immediately after our interview he went straight back to his plants.

Nice work if you can get it: After his retirement, John hadn't trained for eight months when a club rang wanting him to sit on the bench as cover for a few games. He rejected the idea because a second choice keeper has to be fully fit and alert in case he is needed. He may not have played many games in his second spell at Arsenal but he never cheated the Gunners out of a day's hard graft.

I bet he hates that David Seaman though: How can you dislike David Seaman? They are good friends.

But he kept John out of action at Arsenal? When Seaman was a young keeper at Leeds, John was in his first spell there and automatic first choice. Manager Eddie Gray off-loaded Seaman to Peterborough and later the wheel turned full circle as Seaman kept Lukic on the bench for long spells at Highbury.

Did you know? John won championships at Leeds and Arsenal and was the first Leeds player to cost £1million when he returned from Arsenal in 1990.

Urban myth: Lukic did not survive the Munich Air Crash. It would have been difficult. The crash happened in 1958 and John wasn't born until 1960.

Lives: Chesterfield. Whether he will eventually be tempted back into football as a coach or manager remains to be seen, but at the moment he is perfectly happy in his garden.

Paul Madeley

Age: 61.
Appearance: Merchant banker.
Joined Leeds: 1962.
Games: 708 (34 goals).
Bookings: 2.
A rare commodity: The only club he played for was Leeds.
England appearances: 24, despite turning down a place in Alf Ramsey's squad for the 1970 World Cup squad after a long hard season with Leeds.
Nickname: The Rolls Royce. He played in every position except keeper with the elegance and grace of a classic car. Never broke down, always dependable.
Retired: 1980.

Management was not for him: Paul had actually shown a head for business well before he quit the game. He owned a newsagents during his time at Leeds.

And then? When he retired, Paul ran a sports shop in Chapel Allerton (It eventually changed into a ladies fashion shop). The big time came when he entered the family DIY business, based in Yorkshire and the South West. His brother John was a driving force behind the chain and they became millionaires when the business was sold in 1987 for £27 million.

A lot of money especially in those days: Paul said the figure was exaggerated but that's what the papers quoted.

No need to work after that: Paul didn't. He bought some shares in Halifax Town but money cannot buy you your health and Paul didn't have the best of luck health wise from the early 90s. Heart problems mainly.

His Rolls Royce needs a new engine: Unfortunately there aren't the new parts available that will cure Parkinson's disease. Paul has been suffering from the disease for some years.

Paul Madeley on Parkinson's: *"Some days are better than others, but there are people far worse off than me. I won't let it get me down."*

Does he think of the old days? He had a framed picture of Leeds' 1972 FA Cup winning side hanging in his office. *"It was an inspiration, just looking at it."*

Lives: Bramhope.

Phil Masinga

Age: 36.
Real name: Philemon Masinga.
Leeds era: 1994-1996.
Arrived from: South African football along with Lucas Radebe. Typical Yorkshire - it was a 2-for-the-price-of-1 offer.
Bold move: It was Howard Wilkinson who signed him after watching him play for Mamelodi Sundowns.
Games: 39 (11 goals).
Position: Up front when Yeboah/Chapman/Deane or Whelan were unavailable.
After Leeds: St. Gallen (Switzerland), Salernitana and

Bari (Italy). He was Bari's top scorer in Series A for 2 seasons. He left Italy in 2001 and signed for Coventry but was not granted a working visa - his reason for leaving Leeds.
Retired: 2002 playing for Al-Wahda in the United Arab Emirates.
Reason for retirement: A knee injury on a knee that had already had two operations.
So back to South Africa? Yes sir. As soon as he returned he began coaching kids at Orlando Stadium and giving talks on AIDS and smoking.
It's a filthy habit: In 2003 he was appointed ambassador for South Africa's bid for the 2010 World Cup finals.
He swapped tracksuit for a suit? Indeedy. Chippa, as he likes to be known, travels the world selling South Africa's sporting infrastructure to members and delegates of FIFA.
You have to be squeaky clean for that job: That's right, but in 2005 he was arrested for drink driving and resisting arrest. His position could be in jeopardy since it is a prison term offence in that part of the world if he's found guilty.
Let's hope he gets a judge who's a Leeds fan: Either that or hires the lawyer who defended Michael Jackson.

Gary McAllister MBE

Born: Motherwell.
Age: 40.
Appearance: Posh hotel manager.
Leeds era: 1990-1996.
Games: 294 (45 goals).
Forte: Ball distribution.
Millionaire's club: McAllister was Leeds' second ever million pound signing.
Sold: To Coventry for £3 million.
Scotland caps: 57.
Other clubs: Motherwell, Leicester, Coventry and Liverpool.
Retired: 2002.
Didn't he go back to

Coventry? Yes as manager. It was a position he held with some success until 2004.

Why leave? He went to look after his ill wife Denise. Gary has kept in touch with football by appearing on Sky as a TV pundit and helps out at SFX, the management company that has looked after his affairs since he started out in professional football. He still plays golf and has a handicap of four.

So what happened to his wife? She is in remission from breast cancer and doing well, but football management is an every minute of every day occupation, so Gary's priority is looking after his wife and he is not ready to return just yet.

Midlands boy: When Gary left Liverpool to rejoin Coventry in 2002 he had kept his house in Leicester and lives there with Denise and sons Jake, 11, and Oliver, 4. When Denise was pregnant with Oliver she delayed chemotherapy until after he was born so there would be no risk to the baby's health from her treatment.

He deserves a medal: He's got plenty. Macca was awarded the MBE in the 2002 New Year Honours List for his services to football. Before joining Liverpool he had won just two medals - the Scottish Division 1 title with Motherwell in 1985 and the League Championship with Leeds in 1992. But in just over a season at Liverpool he won five medals.

What gives him nightmares? The penalty miss in the 1996 European Championships against England.

John McClelland

Age: 50.
Leeds era: 1989-1996.
Looks like: Lee Chapman.
Appearances: 29 (0 goals).
Not many, was he injured? At previous clubs he had a personal training regime but at Leeds his needs were ignored. As soon as he trained with the rest of the team he began to get injured.

Groin strains? Bone spurs.
Position: Centre-half.
Also trained as: A fish factory cockle processor, and a newsagent (aged 9).
Other clubs: Cardiff City, Mansfield, Glasgow Rangers, Watford, Notts County and Darlington.
Retired: At Darlington in 1997.
Reason: He broke his leg in 3 places on his very first appearance for the club.
Did he see out the rest of his contract on crutches? There was no contract signed. John spent the next 12 months convalescing at home in Wakefield.
Watching Trisha and UK Gold? Training to be a house husband. As soon as he could walk he took over the duties of the house for a further 12 months whilst his wife went out to work.
When did he finally get back to work? 2000. The commercial department at Leeds United offered him a full-time job as Tour Manager. He was remembered at Leeds as being approachable and generous with his time. He was perfect to show people around the ground.
What's the most exciting bit? Going into the first team dressing room.
Can I go in at 2:45pm on a Saturday? They're a bit busy then. The tour costs £5 for juniors and £8 for adults and he does tours for kids and businesses. It takes about 2 hours and you're taken to a glass case where some of his 53 Northern Ireland caps are on display.
Any aspirations to become a manager? He is happy coaching kids in his spare time and being a taxi service to his 11-year-old son.
Would we recognise him today? He hasn't changed one bit.

George McCluskey

Age: 48.
Born: Hamilton, Scotland.
Games: 75 (17 goals).
Position: Centre-forward (allegedly).
Strengths: Scoring from twenty yards in the warm-up.
Weaknesses: Not one for chasing lost causes. He didn't have much pace either.
Era: Eddie Gray signed him from Celtic in 1983. He stayed until 1986.
I am surprised to hear he left Celtic for Leeds: Eddie Gray talked him into swapping European football and championship medals for Division 2 action at Elland Road. Plus George was having contractual wrangles with Celtic.
After Leeds: Hibernian, Hamilton Accies, Kilmarnock and Clyde.
Retired: Aged 39.
Then what? In 1997 George began selling forklift trucks in Glasgow. It wasn't easy - forklifts don't exactly need replacing for new models very often but he did well and made it to Sales Manager. In 1999 he later moved into the taxi driving business.
Is his meter still running? Yes but he's not as full-on as he used to be since he is also a youth coach at Celtic. The club has 10 development centres in Glasgow and he runs the Glasgow South depot.
Does he get flagged down? George is still a hero to half the city so he has to be careful who he picks up. He wouldn't want Graeme Souness in the back of his cab.
Why? Graeme tried to amputate his leg during a match in 1990. It went on to be voted the worst tackle ever seen on Scottish TV. It still gives George nightmares.
Hobbies: Golf.
Is he a Leeds fan? Not exactly, but he does look out for the results and the McCluskey clan loved their time at Leeds – a very nice place and the people were really friendly. The family home was in Wetherby and George used to play a fair bit of snooker with Andy Ritchie in the local working men's club.

Bobby McDonald

Age: 50
Looks like? Phil Collins.
Games: 24 (1 goal - against Ipswich Town).
Era: 1987-1988.
Strengths: Tackling, passing, attacking from deep.
Signed for Leeds aged: 32. Bremner wanted some youth in the side.
Low point? He was so distraught at losing the play-off final in 1987 that he threw his entire strip to the Leeds fans as an apology for the defeat.
Other clubs: Aston Villa, Coventry City, Manchester City, Oxford United and Wolves.
Retired: 1988.

Rumour had it: Bobby would death-stare his opponents. It's a tactic he even used in training.

Sounds like he'd make a good manager? Perhaps, but he wasn't interested. Once he'd packed in playing, that was it, end of story. He moved back to his home town of Aberdeen.

And did he find work? In 1992 he joined the Scottish Ambulance Service, helping to transport patients around the country. He did that for 5 years.

Did he see some horrific scenes? It's not like what you see on Casualty. He was more taking home patients and picking up another to put in the bed newly vacated by the patient he'd just driven away. A bit of organ transportation too.

So in 1997: He was on the dole. He later worked for a builders merchant and for a company called 'Lifestyle', who sold steam capsules - a kind of innovative shower portal – but they went bust.

He isn't having much luck: Finally, he moved south to Mansfield, where he lives today. He saw a newspaper advertisement for a job as a TV rigger. They provide the technical equipment for TV companies filming outside broadcast programmes. He gets to travel a bit but he's normally stuck in TV compounds.

Billy McGhie

Age: 47.
Height: 7' 3" if you include the hair.
Appearance: Honorary president of the Candy Floss Association.
Position: Forward.
Era: 1976-1979.
Games: 2 (1 goal – on his debut against Ipswich).
That's not a lot of action: In those days nobody was allowed to get out their knitting whilst waiting for a game. He played every week for the reserves.
Billy on football: *"I tried to enjoy my life as a player as*

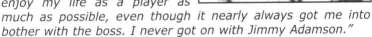

much as possible, even though it nearly always got me into bother with the boss. I never got on with Jimmy Adamson."
After Leeds: Aged just 21 Billy was sent packing (by Adamson not surprisingly). He ended up going to York City.
Retired: 1982.
Then what? Billy went to play in Denmark for Boldspilklub but after a couple of months he became homesick and returned home. An illustrious career over.
After football? He's had various jobs over the years, including roofing work in Germany, agricultural labour (working in fields) and working in betting shops. His latest job is working behind the counter in a bookies, taking the bets while occasionally handing winnings back to punters.
Maths wise is he good enough to go on 'Countdown'? He says he isn't as the machines do all the work for you.
Lives: Rossington, near Doncaster.
Is he still a 'redhead'? Yes, what there is left of it. He looks like a circus clown.
Hobbies: Watching his son William play football as well as following most sports, especially horse racing.
High hopes: William actually starts an apprenticeship with Scunthorpe United in summer 2005. *"He's a quality left-winger and has got good potential".*
Goals in life if not in football? Billy's biggest ambition is that his son William will make it big-time as a pro. You probably wouldn't want to bet against it.

John McGoldrick

Age: 42.
Born: Scotland.
Leeds era: 1983-1985.
Another Eddie Gray signing from Scotland: This one only played 12 games though. Still, he didn't cost anything and he paid his own fare down from Glasgow.
Goals: None.
Position: Right back.
High point: *"I cannot remember".*
Debut: *"I cannot remember".* (It was against Chester in 1983).
He doesn't remember much:

We caught him on a busy day and it was twenty years ago when he played
Other clubs: Celtic and Motherwell.
Retired: 1985 aged 22.
That's young: He had five operations on a troublesome knee. Four of those operations were at Celtic (the first when he was aged just 17) and one for good measure when he got to Leeds. Although he moved north of the border after Leeds he never actually played again.
Was he put down? In Footballing terms he was but he then moved into the car selling business in Airdrie. His family owned two dealerships in the area and he worked in one of them for just under a year.
Then what? His big break. He moved to a car dealership company called Arnold Clark at Bishopbriggs near Glasgow and he has been there ever since. That was 1986.
What does he do? He's the General Manager specialising in Renault cars.
Does he see any of the former players? Only George McCluskey. He went to John Donnelly's 40th birthday party a few years back but we got the impression John wanted to forget about football altogether.
You mean he'd rather talk cars? He wouldn't really talk about anything other than his knee operations.
How are his knees today? Not great. After all the operations they look like a template for playing noughts and crosses.

John McGovern

Born: Montrose.
Age: 55.
Leeds era: August 1974 to February 1975.
Games: Four.
Not many: He was dubbed as 'Cloughie's Envoy' and when Cloughie got the boot there wasn't much room for 'old stiff arms'.
Style: He ran like he was wearing far too many layers of clothing under a brand new denim jacket.
Goals: None.
Position: Midfield.
Other clubs: Hartlepool, Derby,

Nottingham Forest, Bolton (player-manager), Horwich RMI, Chorley (manager), Plymouth (assistant manager), Rotherham (joint manager with Archie Gemmill), Hull City (assistant manager) and Woking (manager).
Mr Motivator: Having risen through all four divisions inside 18 months and gone on to lift the European Cup twice, John is well qualified for one of his present jobs as a motivational expert.
You say it's <u>one</u> of his jobs: Like Norman Hunter at Leeds, John combines everything with being a host at Nottingham Forest's home matches. Another of his jobs is selling wine for wine merchants - a real labour of love!
I'd say his Leeds vintage would be made from sour grapes: Perhaps. His time at Leeds was the longest 7 months of his footballing career but he went on to bigger and better things.
Working for a living: John and his partner Ann have lived in Sheffield for the last ten years but he worked for an estate agency (not Timeshare he hastens to point out) in Tenerife and eventually went independent. He lived in Tenerife for four years after leaving Bolton where he was player-manager from 1982 to 1984. He also managed a services company in South Manchester that did cutlery packing and laundry for airlines.
The Clough/Leeds thing: Some players wouldn't accept Brian Clough. It was a nightmare for McGovern who eventually rejoined Clough at Forest where his career took off again.

Duncan McKenzie

Age: 55.
Position: Striker.
Era: 1974-1976. He was signed by Brian Clough.
Fans would say: 'Entertaining'.
Players would say: 'Greedy'.
Played for: Notts Forest, Mansfield (loan), Leeds, Anderlecht, Everton, Chelsea, Blackburn, Tulsa Roughnecks and Chicago Stings.
Party piece: Jumping over mini cars and throwing golf balls the length of a football pitch. In his Forest days Duncan used to leap over a 5ft gate, with barbed wire on the top (ouch), on his way

back from training runs near the River Trent. That ensured he was quickest to arrive back, so he didn't miss out on a drink of cool lemon.
So legend has it: Reserve keeper Brian Williamson reckoned that if Duncan could clear the fence he would have no trouble jumping over Tommy Cavanagh's mini. He would have to be shot from a cannon to do it today.
I'll bet managers pulled their hair out over him: A few did. Once, he had three managers in one day at Chelsea.
Retired: 1983.
After football: Wife Dot had a flower shop while Duncan was playing football, so as soon as he retired he joined in the business, selling flowers, fruit and veg. They later opened another shop in Prescott, Liverpool.
I've heard he's very much the media darling: In the mid 80s he became the flavour of the month, doing radio commentaries, TV appearances and writing a national newspaper column.
He's in demand? Nowhere more than on the after-dinner circuit. He's one of the main attractions and a big draw.
Is it just football seminars he does? No he does business after-dinners, golf after-dinners, after-dinners to mixed audiences...you name it he does it. It has been his full-time occupation for 15 years.
His way of life is: *"Utopia - much better than going down the mine or sailing on a Grimsby trawler."*

David McNiven

Age: 50.
Appearance: A stocky man with brillo pads stuck to the side of his face.
Leeds era: 1971-1978.
Main asset: Speed.
High point: Just being part of the first team squad.
Other clubs: Bradford, Blackpool and Halifax. He also had a spell playing in America in 1984.
Retired: 1985.
Then what? Milkman.
Pull the udder one? Seriously. In 1986 David began a milk round in St. Anne's, Lancashire.

He was the fastest milkman in the west.

Faster than Ernie? After a year of the early mornings he went to work for Evans Halshaw in Preston as a second-hand car salesman. Fords mainly. Capris, Escorts and Granadas.

How did he get into that? With no other skills, he applied for the job, the company took him on, trained him and he was very good. He went on to be 'Salesman of the Year' on two occasions. He lived in the area too so the job was perfect.

Any urges to move back to Leeds? He married a Leeds lass and visits on family occasions but has only been back to Elland Road once.

Does he have any interests in the game? He has twin sons aged 26, who play professionally. Scott with Mansfield, and David with Queen of the South.

Where is David today? Still at Evans Halshaw in Preston. He's the Commercial Sales Manager. He's been with the company 18 years and now runs a department of 9 other salesmen and 2 administrators. This year's target is to off-load 1100 vans.

Did he try and sell you anything over the phone? No but he did ask me for Carl Harris's phone number. He's lived in the same house for 22 years so maybe he needed some furniture moving? Carl Harris used to live opposite David in Drighlington.

What did he do with his old sock tabs? Does he use them like furry dice in his car? He's kept a few shirts but they would cover up too much of the windscreen. He doesn't know where the sock tabs are.

Gordon McQueen

Age: 53
Leeds era: 1972-1978.
Games: 171 (19 goals).
Shirt number: 5.
House proud: During his time at Leeds, Gordon lived in the former home of Pete Stringfellow.
Retired: 1985.
Other clubs: St Mirren and Manchester United, Seiko (Hong Kong) as player/coach, Airdrieonians as manager, returned to St Mirren as coach, Middlesbrough and first team coach.

The Sky's the limit: Big Gordon is one of Sky TVs busiest presenters. He can turn his hand to co-commentary or studio work and completed around 70 shows during the 2004/5 season. You can spot him as he sometimes wears odd coloured suits.

Ankle deep in pain: Like so many ex-footballers, he is now paying the physical price for years of being patched up to defy injuries and returned to the city of Leeds in May for major ankle surgery.

Across the Pennines: Gordon can sympathise with Alan Smith and Rio Ferdinand who have been pilloried by Leeds fans for defecting to Manchester United. Gordon and Joe Jordan were criticised for their move across the Pennines, though the feeling of resentment by the fans didn't run quite so deep.

It's a shame: Gordon and Joe are rarely invited back to Elland Road for functions and Gordon suspects their Manchester United connection is the reason.

It's good to talk: Gordon and Joe speak on the phone at least twice a week. *"Hello Joe, goodbye, Joe."*

Yorkshire base: After spending seven years coaching at Middlesbrough, Gordon left in 1991 and has continued living in North Yorkshire. He went straight into TV work at Sky after quitting his job as manager of part-timers Airdrieonians from 1987 to 1989. At one time he ran a greetings card shop in Paisley but was never cut out to stand behind a counter.

Family: He and his wife Yvonne have two grown up daughters and a son.

Jon Newsome

Age: 35.
Born: Sheffield.
Leeds era: 1991-1994.
Position: At the back.
Although a defender: He's probably best known for scoring the second goal against Sheffield United which contributed to Leeds winning the 1991/92 title.

What he liked about Leeds: *"The players we had at that time were a great bunch of lads. Both talented and personable."*

How will he be known at Leeds as a player? *"I do not know. It is for the fans to say what sort of a player I was but I gave it my best shot."*

Other clubs: Sheffield Wednesday, Norwich and Bolton.

Retired: 2000 due to knee injury. Today he's a successful motor trader in Sheffield with his own company called AutoMarques.

He was telling me: *"I buy cars from dealers and sell them on. I bid for a Bentley GT the other day but missed out."*

It hasn't always been the case: Although Jon set up the business 18-months ago he has had a few other jobs before now.

Such as: His first job after football was as a financial advisor. It took him 2/3 years to become qualified but he didn't much like it when he was cast into the great big world. Then he worked as a sales rep for a sports equipment firm. Luckily his love of cars has come up trumps with www.automarques.com. His job involves a bit of financing so his college studies are not a complete waste of time.

What about football? Jon hoped to stay in the game when he quit but it was tough. He has his coaching badge and in 2002 became the manager of Gresley Rovers who play in the Dr Martens League.

What happened? After a year he had to leave for personal reasons. He doesn't even do any kids coaching these days.

Who did Jon room with in the glory days? Mervyn Day. Although he wasn't the first choice at the club, the two got on great.

John O Hare

Born: Dumbarton.
Age: 58.
Leeds era: August 1974 to February 1975.
Games: 7 (1 goal - away at Coventry).
Position: Striker.
Other clubs: Sunderland, Derby, Nottingham Forest, Dallas Tornado (NASL), Belper Town, Derby Carriage and Wagon FC, Ockbrook FC, Stanton (manager), Leicester City (scout) and Celtic (scout).
Retired from football league: 1980.
Scotland caps: 13.

Scout's honour: John still watches Leeds from time to time in his job as a scout for Celtic. He gets to more Championship matches than Premiership games because it's easier to get players to leave for Scotland from that league than the Premiership.

What's his position now Martin O'Neill is no longer at Celtic? He scouted for Martin O'Neill at Leicester before O'Neill moved to Celtic. Now he is working for Gordon Strachan in the same role, though he has continued living in Derby.

Medallion man: John won a European Championship winners medal after leaving Leeds for Nottingham Forest and enjoyed great success under Brian Clough's management. He had won a League Championship winners medal under Clough at Derby and was taken to Leeds by Clough in 1974.

O'Hare on Clough at Leeds: *"It was never going to work with Clough as manager because the Leeds players had grown up with Don Revie, and Brian had a totally different way of managing."*

Away from football: O'Hare ran a pub near Derby for ten months but he and his wife felt it was the wrong environment in which to bring up kids. He enjoyed working for steel erectors at International Combustion in Derby and then as a stock controller at Toyota's European plant on the outskirts of the town.

Family: John and his wife have three daughters, a son and six grandchildren. His son, also called John, played for Grantham and Grimsby but didn't make the grade.

David O Leary

Age: 47.
Leeds era: 1993-1995.
Appearance: Laid back and nice but hiding a temper that would set off a stampede of elephants.
Joined Leeds: From Arsenal in 1993.
Games: Just 10.
Not many: He will be remembered as a manager of Leeds not a player.
Caps: 66 (Republic of Ireland)
Retired: 1995 (injury).
Did Howard Wilkinson have a heart? He surely did. Due to his wealth of experience, O'Leary was kept on as defence coach.

In the days where you had a coach for every position? Seemingly. David was coaching the reserves too until 1996 when George Graham took over as manager. He immediately appointed O'Leary as his assistant.

But George jumped ship? GG went to Spurs in 1998 but after a knock-back from first choice Martin O'Neill, O'Leary got the job as Leeds manager.

What followed? Success of sorts. Although he never won anything, his team consisting of the Leeds babes had 4 successive seasons in the top 5 of the Premiership. Only in 2002 was he sacked when Leeds failed to get into the Champions League.

Seems a bit harsh: If we still had O'Leary we would still be in the Premier League.

Then what happened? For legal reasons he was out of the game for nine months before becoming manager of Aston Villa in 2003. He is still there in 2005 and signed a contract to keep him at the club until 2007.

Money in the bank: £7 million and counting.

Books: 'Leeds United On Trial'. An account of the 2000/2001 season in which Leeds hit the headlines for so many reasons.

Least likely to say: *"I've got an idea for another book."*

2005 Controversy: On the back of the tapping up of Ashley Cole, O'Leary is likely to face his own tapping up scandal when the FA investigate the approach made to James Beattie.

'Tapping up' goes on all the time: O'Leary agrees.

Brendan Ormsby

Age: 45.
Born: Birmingham.
Appearance: George Formby on steroids.
Position: Centre-half.
Games: 56 (7 goals).
Strengths: Heading.
Signed from: Aston Villa, 1985.
Leeds high point? Getting to the FA Cup semis & play-off finals in 1987.
Low point: Brendan has never been afraid of taking the blame for a crucial goal in that semi-final against Coventry. He also badly damaged his knee ligaments in the play-off final. He had two seasons out of the game and it effectively ended his Leeds career.
After Leeds: Shrewsbury (1 game, 1990), Doncaster (1990), Scarborough (1992), Waterford (1993-4) and Wigan (1994-5).
Retired: 1995.
Did his knees finally give out? No, it was actually worse than that. While playing amateur football for Garforth Town he began getting headaches and double vision. His doctor told him if he carried on heading the ball there was a chance the blood vessels behind his eyes would burst and he'd lose his sight.
Blimey: Well Brendan loves playing and can't resist the occasional kick-about with the Leeds ex-players team (which he runs, too). He doesn't head the ball as much as he used to.
Workwise? He regularly hosts a phone-in show for *Real Radio* in Leeds and is also a Match Co-ordinator for the Press Association, passing on news and statistics to the commentary teams. Oh, and he's a postman too.
Postman! We're always getting our neighbour's mail: The Post Office made £450 million last year and Brendan has perfect eyesight so you can't blame him. He offers a first class service.
Where's his patch? Moortown (or LS8) and he actually delivers to his own house (LS17).
Does he deliver much junk mail? Only to a neighbour who gets the Manchester United magazine.

Carlton Palmer

Age: 40.
Appearance: The village idiot of a town where only basketball players are allowed to live.
Leeds era: 1994-1997.
Games: 130 (7 goals).
Position: Centre half (probably his better position) and midfield (probably his worst position).
Role: To give away the ball and free-kicks in highly dangerous areas.

But are we not talking about Carlton Palmer the England international? He's the same person, getting 18 caps for his country. It was all under Graham Taylor's reign so it doesn't really count.
Other clubs: He played for five different Premier League clubs - Sheffield Wednesday, Leeds, Southampton, Nottingham Forest and Coventry.
Retired: 2001.
And? On to management what else. His final league club as a player was Stockport and they gave him his first taste of soccer management in 2001. In the same season they were relegated. After narrowly missing out on being relegated from Division 2 in 2003, a poor start to the 2003/04 season confirmed Carlton was on his way by taxi.
By taxi? Carlton can't drive. Well he can but isn't allowed to. In 2001 he was banned for two years for drink-driving. At Leeds he was in court on a similar offence but got off on a technicality.
In the dock: Carlton's no stranger to court appearances and he actually sued Stockport for unfair dismissal and won. He got a full 12-months wages as compensation which was about £50.
Fitness: Whilst he was waiting for the tribunal to run its course he kept himself fit by playing for Dublin City.
Back in the hot seat? Carlton was appointed manager of Mansfield Town in November 2004 and is still there.
But for how long? They finished the 2004/05 season in mid-table in Division 2 so he's safe for now.
Mansfield. Is their ladies team called Womansfield? No.
Lives: Near Sheffield.
Sinner: He likes the odd tab.

Keith Parkinson

Age: 49.
Era: 1973-1982.
Games: 38.
Goals: None, although he did hit the post in one match.
Keith claims: *"I played more reserve games than any other Leeds player."*
Other clubs: Hull and Doncaster.
Retired: 1982 at Doncaster where manager Billy Bremner told him he had no future in football. He was aged just 26.
So Keith took Bremner's advice? Yes. He didn't even consider playing for another

club. Indirectly though Bremner was right. It led to D-Day. 7 March 1983 was the day Keith Parkinson made the best decision of his life.

He signed for Real Madrid? He joined the police force. Keith Parkinson became PC Parkinson or PC 2864.

Was he in uniform? His first posting was at Milgarth, Leeds, where he walked the beat. He was there for 6 years before being transferred to Pudsey.

What was he doing? Apprehending the undesirables of this world. He often did police duty down at Elland Rd but the only person to recognise him was Peter Lorimer.

Did he feel many collars? Pudsey was a safer place to be but after 12 years on duty, in 2000, Keith joined the neighbourhood police team at Dewsbury nick.

Still in uniform? Still wearing the gear even though he has to buy his own boots unlike his days at Leeds.

Is that where he is today? Yes, covering Cleckheaton and Batley.

How long has he served? 22 years so he could retire in 3 years time.

Has he any awards for bravery? No. His only award has been for good attendance. He hasn't missed a day in 12 years.

So how will he spend his days when he finishes in the police? Tending to his large garden in New Farnley, doing a bit of DIY. He has the level 2 coaching badge that he puts to good use these days taking charge of Thornes FC Under-15s.

Derek Parlane

Age: 52.
Era: Early 1980s.
Position: Centre forward.
A goal scorer? Only 10 goals in 3 seasons.

That's a drought: Some fans could have sued under the Trade Description Act. He did plenty of legwork for others to get on the score sheet.
So he was rubbish? More unlucky. It was a transitional period for Leeds in those days.
I suppose we've had worse? Derek actually scored on his debut but remembers the 'Adamson Out' banners held up by fans more than anything. Three managers in as many seasons didn't help his game, plus a bad injury.
Pity: Anyway, in order to get back to match fitness, he went on loan to Hong Kong in 1983 and there met a Dutch businessman who was to become his saviour when he retired.
When was retirement? In 1988 at Macclesfield Town.
Any coaching? *"When you quit the game, you quit the game".* That's when the Oriental connection kicked in.
Did he star in a kung fu movie? He began selling sports clothing. 1988 was the year of becoming a self-employed Sales Agent. His Dutch friend manufactured goods in Hong Kong and when they needed a distributor in the UK, they turned to Derek.
I suppose it is better than nothing: He had nothing else so he took up the offer and started selling O'Neill's clothing before it became trendy.
Just O'Neill's? Another imported brand, Russell Athletic, thought Derek was so good they appointed him their Sales Agent in 1992. Then in 1996, he was poached by Reebok to be the UK Sales Manager and he has been there ever since.
So that's where the football background comes in? He is responsible for Reebok kits at Liverpool (the longest Premiership shirt/sponsor partnership). He makes sure the retail outlets work in tandem with the Reebok brand.
Lives: Lytham St. Anne's and is married to Julie
Likes: Tennis, gardening and golf.

John Pearson

Age: 42.
Height: 6' 2"
Era: 1987-1991.
Bought from: Charlton for £70,000.
Position: Striker.
Aka: 'Big Bird'.
Role: To stand in the opponents half and wait for the ball to land on his head.
Games: 121 (12 goals).
Myth: That Arthur C. Clarke was commissioned to make a documentary on how Big John got in the team.
Guilty: He's centre forward in the worst Leeds team.

After Leeds: Barnsley, Hull City (loan), Cardiff, Chorley and Sheffield Wednesday (for 1 game).
Just one game? The Owls were short of a striker and gave Pearson a game. It was a European game too so he had his European debut, team debut and final game at the same time.
Retired? 1995.
Who advised him to take this drastic action? The fans? Big John always got on well with the fans since he gave 100%. Doctors ultimately told him to find another profession after persistent neck complaints.
What next then? He took a course in mortgage consultancy with Abbey National, and did the obligatory school coaching.
And? In 1997 he took over as manager of Sheffield FC (the oldest league team in England). That lasted for 3 seasons after taking them as far as they could go. He worked for a football agent business too, but was made redundant. During this time he also bought a café near Hillsborough, with his wife.
How many Michelin stars did it have? It's hard to get any serving egg and chips. It was a 'greasy spoon' but it did okay and they sold it 3 years later for a small profit. He didn't leave the catering business altogether since they own another in Spittal Hill, Sheffield.
Nowadays: He works as a mortgage consultant for financial services company Cattles. He also does his bit for Sheffield Wednesday as a match summariser for BBC Radio Sheffield.

John Pemberton

Age: 40.
Leeds era: 1993-1997.
Games: 67 (0 goals)
No goals! Even Paul Robinson scored for Leeds? John was a committed defender.
Other clubs: Rochdale, Crewe (twice), Crystal Palace, Sheffield United and Nottingham Forest (Assistant Academy Manager).
Retired: 1998.
Injury: Pembo's playing career was virtually ended by a knee injury suffered at Leeds. In 1997 Dario Gradi took him on for a second spell at Crewe as player/coach. Then, in what

turned out to be a one-match comeback, he broke down and decided enough was enough.
And so to coaching? John was taken to Nottingham Forest by Paul Hart. When Hart was taking the Under-19s, John had charge of the Under-15s to Under-17s and is now the club's Assistant Academy Manager. He is responsible for structuring from Under-9 to Under-19 level and holds a UEFA 'A' coaching license, the highest level in Europe.
Good lad: Pembo was popular with Leeds fans for his fully committed attitude and, despite injury problems, he feels he produced the best football of his career at Elland Road until George Graham released him.
He has a lot to answer for does that Mr Graham: Not until we spoke to John for this book had anyone from Leeds United been in touch to enquire about his welfare and he feels strongly that he was left to fend for himself with a young family to support.
So what about Forest? They've just been relegated into Division 1: John is heartened that the backroom staff are keeping their jobs and will be given a chance to get the club promoted at the first attempt. He enjoys working with young players, especially at Forest, a club that has long had a high reputation on the youth side.
Family: Wife and 2 sons.
Pals: Chris Fairclough and Paul Beesley are close friends. They all work for Forest and live in the Sheffield area.

Terry Phelan

Age: 38.
Leeds era: 1984-1986.
Appearance: Trainee swimming pool attendant.
Games: 19.
Position: Left back by default.
Why's that? He played on the wing originally but Eddie Gray shoved him to left back when Leeds had an injury crisis. He never looked back.

He got a name for himself once he left Leeds: He's probably best known for his time at Wimbledon and Manchester City.
International caps: 41 (Republic of Ireland).
Retired: 2001 at Sheffield United aged just 34.
What did he do for work? He had offers to extend his career in the UK but his CV was touted about in America and he got a 2-year contract playing for a team called Charleston Battery down in South Carolina.
How did that go down with the Phelan's? Fine. Wife and three kids all loved it and Terry played well. In his second year, the team's goalkeeper, Todd Hoffard, invited him to visit his One-on-One soccer school in Philadelphia. It was a summer camp for American kids and soon enough Terry was offered a job to partner Todd as Director of Football which he accepted in 2004.
So what happens there? Parents pay for their kids to reside at the camps and they get professional football coaching. At any one time they will have 250 kids to look after and Terry employs many ex-pros from the UK.
Sounds like a logistical nightmare? It can be hectic and Terry's business now travels across the States doing summer and holiday football camps. He is spending the summer of 2005 in Alaska.
Does he have a base back in the UK? No. He sold up lock, stock and barrel. He used to have two homes in Florida but now lives the simple life.
Hates: Parents and Disneyland.
Where seen: Having a pint in an Irish bar in Philly.

Paul Reaney

Age: 61.
Nickname: 'Speedy'.
Position: Right-back.
Speciality: Overlapping and goal line clearances.
Era: 1961-1978.
A rare breed: His whole career was spent with virtually the one club.

Didn't he also play for Bradford City? He went on to play 38 times in the late 1970s but he was way past his best.
Retired: In 1980 but he went to Australia and carried on playing for a team called Newcastle Jets in 1981. That lasted 2 years in which time Paul started coaching.
Always good to get some coaching on your CV: In 1983 Paul returned to the UK and began working for International World of Sport (IWS).
Does he know Dickie Davis? Don't get confused with the Saturday afternoon TV show. IWS organised football coaching at holiday camps.
Ho-De-Ho: Pontin's and Butlin's. Paul still based himself in Knaresborough and drove all over the country doing 1700 miles a week visiting 22 different centres. He worked the camps for 17 years until 2000.
He must be fit? He looks very trim.
Did he stop coaching? Not entirely. He still does coaching at Potters in Great Yarmouth. Every school holiday he is down there teaching the kids everything he learned from Don Revie.
What does he do when the kids are at school? A big part of Paul's life now revolves around a business called 'Golden Era'.
Sounds good? Since 2000 Paul has pooled together all the old Revie lads and coordinates their work and appearances. They're in great demand.
He's an agent? More like a representative. There are 20 players and he does most of their commercial deals from supermarket openings to after-dinners and books.
How would I get into his good books? Buy him some aftershave.
And when it's cold: He jets off to his 'little place in Spain'.

David Rennie

Age: 41.
Leeds era: 1986-1989.
Bought/sold: Bremner/ Wilkinson.
Games: 109 (6 goals).
Appearance: Conservative MP.
Position: Midfield and centre-back.
Retired: 1999 at Peterborough United
Retired (semi-pro): 2000 at Boston United.
Was he ready for retirement? In some ways. In the twilight of his career he started attending courses that would hopefully give him some skills in the outside world.

Like what? He started selling insurance part-time to see if he would like it. He didn't. Then he went to college part-time.
What did he study? Marketing, PR and Spanish. He also took a couple of courses in IT.
What exactly is IT? Information Technology. David said it was *"programming, spread sheets and databases"*.
He should apply to be Alan Sugar's next Apprentice: In 2000 he got a job with a small IT company in Leicester. He wouldn't say who they were and we did ask.
He's not giving much away. In 2001 he joined another company called Croner Consultants based in Leicester. He's been there ever since.
What's his job title? He's not sure. "Something between IT and sales" he thinks. He advises businesses on health and safety issues and employment law. He is on the road quite a bit so selling must be a big part of his day. When we spoke to him he was in Norfolk.
Hobbies: The gym and learning Spanish.
Pre-football ambition: To be an accountant.
Rennie on careers: *"I decided not to go into football management because I had it ruling my life when I was a player."*
Lives: Leicester with wife and 3 kids.

Andy Ritchie

Age: 45.
Position: Striker.
Leeds era: 1983-1987.
Games: 158 (44 goals).

Hate to mention it but... In his Manchester United days, Andy scored a hat-trick against Leeds - but there were no hard feelings when he arrived at Elland Road from Brighton in exchange for Terry Connor.

Champers on ice: Andy kept a bottle of champagne in the fridge for over a year, hoping to crack it open once his contract dispute with Leeds was over, but he continued playing on a week by week agreement before joining Oldham for a bargain £50,000 in 1987.

Other clubs: Manchester United, Brighton, Oldham and Scarborough.

Beside the seaside: Andy's management career started at Scarborough where he was player/coach after leaving Oldham.

Back to Oldham: In 1997 Neil Warnock took Andy back to the Latics as his player/assistant. Then, when Warnock was sacked in 1998, Andy had three seasons as manager. He saved them from relegation and in the next two seasons they finished tenth and eleventh.

And to Leeds: When he got the bullet at Oldham in 2001, Andy was out of work for three months before Peter Ridsdale asked him to become Leeds' Academy Director, with Brian Kidd's blessing.

Chop and change: When Peter Reid became Leeds manager in 2003, Andy lost his job. Six months later Ridsdale, who by this time had taken over at Barnsley, came knocking again. Andy became Academy Manager for the 'Lamb Chops' and when Paul Hart succeeded Gudjon Thordarson as boss, Andy was given more duties, eventually being made first team coach. Although Ridsdale has since departed, Hart and Ritchie were still there.

You say 'were'? In the Spring of 2005, Andy was promoted to caretaker manager when Paul Hart left Barnsley by mutual consent. That became permanent in May 2005.

Home front: Wife Sharon and sons Scott, 16, and Gregg, 20.

David Robertson

Age: 37.
Looks like: Actor Robert Carlisle.
Leeds era: 1997-2000.
Position: Full back.
Signed from: Rangers.
Games: 31.
Why so few? The dreaded curse, injury. David tore his knee pretty badly against Leicester City in 2000 and never played again.
Retired: 2000.
That's the risk those guys take: He tells us he only just passed the medical when he came to Leeds and had been

playing with troublesome knees for 5 years before the injury. He was an accident waiting to happen.
Is that his excuse? Once Ian Harte came into the side his days were numbered. Injury probably did everyone a favour.
Why? Well it prompted David to move into the recycling business which at one point was employing 70 staff.
What did he recycle? Computers. He was based in Wetherby and started it from scratch. He wouldn't give out details of the name of the company but sold it 2 years later for a tidy sum.
So what's he doing now? He's manager of Scottish Division 3 side Elgin City.
How did he get up there? He's from that part of the world anyway and initially moved up to coach Montrose but the offer came to manage Elgin and he took it in 2003.
Robertson on Elgin: *"We're hoping to do a Callie Thistle and get into the Scottish Premier."*
I imagine a club like that is run on a tight budget? David is in charge of 18 full-time players on various government schemes and 15 part-timers.
Any regrets about leaving the computer recycling business? None. He loves the buzz of football management but knows if things go belly-up he can recycle his recycling skills.

David Rocastle

DOB: 1968.
Middle name: Carlyle.
Joined Leeds: From Arsenal in 1992. Howard Wilkinson bought him to add quality to the side after they had won the League title in 1992.

What they said: *"He passed the ball when he should have shot, and shot when he should have passed. He was brilliant."* Don Howe, typically.
Appearance: Member of dance troupe 'Hot Gossip'.
An England International? He won 14 caps for England as well as a League Championship in 1989 and again in 1991.
So he had the class: Yes but he also had a knee injury which limited his appearances.
How many? 34 matches in 18 months.
Curiously: He only scored 2 goals for Leeds – against clubs he would subsequently join.
Other clubs: Manchester City, Chelsea, Norwich, Hull City and Chelsea.
Retired from UK football: 1997.
Abroad: He was the first big name export to bolster the Malaysian league. He signed up for a team called Sabah in 1999.
An odd choice of country to ply your trade: It was a money thing. He lasted a season but injury forced him to quit the game for good and he headed back to the UK in 2000. He's fondly remembered.
Sadly though: David Rocastle's health declined dramatically and he was diagnosed with cancer in 2000. In early 2001 he began the chemotherapy but within a month he had died. He left a wife and 3 kids but his death brought about an awareness of the illness (lymphoma) and a trust was set up in his name.
The day football stood still possibly: It was indeed a black armband day. Ian Wright cried live on radio when he heard the news and tributes flew in from everyone who knew him.

Rocastle passed away March 31, 2001, aged 33.

Ian Rush

Age: 43.
Leeds era: 1996-1997.
Games: 43 (3 goals).
Other clubs: Chester (twice – as a player and manager), Liverpool (twice as a player and once as a coach), Juventus, Newcastle and Wrexham (player/coach).

Rushy the coach: Ian is currently completing his pro coaching license, which has taken four years of study.
Passing the time between jobs: Golfing and horse racing, two of his passions, have had to take a back seat while he concentrates on the coaching course. Still pencil slim, he makes time to go running most mornings and plays in testimonials.
Job offers: A couple of job offers have come in since Ian left Chester City in April 2005 but he wants to be fully qualified on the coaching side before taking his next managerial post.
Ian's way: Ian went back to his first club Chester City as manager in August 2004 with the aim of keeping them in the League and succeeded. *"I now know I can do the job but I left because I wanted to do things my way."*
As manager surely it is his job to do things his way: Rush reckons the owner was undermining his strategy but to be honest results were not going his way and prior to leaving they had just been thumped 5-0 by Shrewsbury.
The goals dried up at Leeds: George Graham played him out of position wide on the right. Rush insists he enjoyed his time at Elland Road but George Graham said he wasn't wanted.
Why did he go to Leeds? To learn from the master tactician Howard Wilkinson.
Awards: Welsh Sports Personality of the Year in 1984. Second was Gwyneth the sheep dog.
Is there another goal Rush on the horizon? Jonathan, at 16 the elder of Ian's two boys, has been with Wrexham as a striker but took six months out to do his GCSE's. Daniel, aged 12, prefers golf and cricket.

Alex Sabella

Age: 51.
Nationality: Argentine.
Full name: Alejandro Sabella.
Appearance: A Latin lover who has to shave three times a day.
Position: Attacking midfield.
Era: 1980-1982.
Other British club: Sheffield United (1978-1980).
Arrived as: Argentina were becoming the most dominant force in world football. He was the first Argentinian to play his club football in England.
Was he like Maradona? Maradona hadn't had his first sniff of coke when Sabella

arrived. Once they had won the World Cup in 1978 English managers welcomed them with open cheque books.
Was he any good? He was very skilful but suffered on some dodgy surfaces. It was a bit physical for slightly built Alex.
Games: 27 (2 goals).
Then what? The Falklands War. Alex opted to leave town. He went back to Argentina to play for Estudiantes (1983-1985), Gremio in Brazil (1985-1986) and finally back to Estudiantes.
Retired: 1987.
Did he return to the UK and manage Halifax Town? Not quite. He went on to be assistant manager at River Plate, one of the biggest clubs in South America. He also had stints as assistant to the Argentine national side until 1998, and the Uruguay national side (1998-2001). In 2001 he was appointed assistant at Parma in Italy, followed by a stint in Mexico.
There's a whole lotta assistant managing going on: All the way through his coaching career he has become the right hand man to fellow Argentine Daniel Passarella. If Passarella became manager, Sabella always became his assistant.
2005: He went to Brazilian side Corinthians. They are the Chelsea of Brazilian football but hate Argentinians. (It would be like Alex Ferguson coming to manage Leeds.) So it is not surprising the two of them were sacked on May 12, 2005, and Sabella went home to sip strong coffee. Rumours have it that one of the players missed a penalty on purpose to hasten the duo's departure.

Scott Sellars

Age: 40.
First club: Leeds.
Not related to: Wine cellars or Big Issue Sellers.
Era: Early 1980s & early 1990s (two spells).
Speciality: Left-footed midfielder. Claims he never scored with his right foot whilst at the club.
What did he do with it? Controlled the ball to a high degree, the likes of which you don't see at the club today.
High point: Debut against Shrewsbury Town and his best goal was a deft little chip (left footed) against Wimbledon.

First Leeds home? He lived with a family in Halton Moor along with John Sheridan, Denis Irwin and Tommy Wright.
Other clubs: Blackburn, Newcastle, Bolton, Huddersfield and Mansfield. In 2001 he had a stint in Denmark playing for AGF.
Retired: 2002 at Mansfield Town.
Then what? Moved back to Sheffield and Tony Daws asked him to coach Sheffield United's Under-9s. His son was there as a promising young attacker so he took the job (Scott actually supports Sheffield Wednesday).
Do the kids call him "Sir"? No, it's Mr Sellars or Scott or Dad. It was a part-time arrangement that allowed him to crack on with other things. Get your passport ready.
Why? Scott is a director of the Brad Friedl Premier School Academy over in Cleveland, America.
Sounds nice: Each summer since 2002, Scott goes over to co-run the residential soccer camp for American kids. I Know What You Did Last Summer Tha' Noz.
And then it's back to sunny Sheffield? Yes. Today, Scott coaches Sheffield United's Under-8s, Under-9s, Under-11s and Under-12s full-time. Sheffield United have an academy a bit like Thorp Arch without the gold taps, and he trains them there. It also involves a lot of evenings and coaching on Sundays for matches.
He won't have time to do much else: No. He gets asked to go back to his various clubs for this and that but says he never has the time. No after-dinners, no golf days, no pubs.

Lee Sharpe

Age: 34.
At Leeds from: 1996-1998.
Appearance: A tramp whose Dad is loaded.
Purchase price: £4.5 million.
Gulp! Not a great investment since he only played 38 times and scored just goals 6 and collected 3 corner flags.
Other clubs: Torquay, Manchester United, Sampdoria (loan), Bradford, Exeter, Portsmouth and Grindavik (Iceland).
Retired: 2003 although he played part-time with Garforth Town.

Assets: He was quick in his playing days and Lee's just as sharp when it comes to spotting a business opportunity. He even took a course in psychology and positive thinking during a long spell out injured at Leeds.
Any new ventures? Lee and a couple of close friends have set up a corporate hospitality company, arranging golfing trips abroad, tickets for international matches and other sporting events. One of their first ventures was a St Patrick's night at Chester FC.
Shucks! I missed that one! Lee also has a property company and until recently he was involved with *The Half Moon* pub at Collingham, near Wetherby.
Did Lee collect glasses? He was a sleeping partner but in 2005 decided pub life wasn't for him and decided to sell up.
Media exposure: He does punditry work but is well down the pecking list but if the money is right would have colonic irrigation on live TV. In the summer of 2005 he came close to winning on Celebrity Love Island. Lee and Abi got on very well.
All good for his tabloid image? Lee's not a tabloid fan after he became the victim of kiss-and-tell revelations. He has lived life to the full but went through a spell of torture when he split from Lisa Crute, his girlfriend of four years, in 1998.
Does he get his tats out for the lads? Lee is probably the only resident of genteel Roundhay with a tattoo of an Indian chief on his right shoulder blade. *"It doesn't mean anything really. He's just a cool Indian."*

John Sheridan

Age: 40.
Not to be confused with: John Sheridan(Writer), John Sheridan (Spurs physio), John Sheridan (Largs Thistle defender).
Nickname: 'Shezzer'.
Appearance: Sunday league football playboy who has bags of talent but still went for a crafty fag at half-time.
Games: 261 (52 goals).
International: 34 (Republic of Ireland)
Strengths: Passing, shooting, free kicks, growing stubble.
Weakness: Tackling.
Era: 1982-1989.

After Leeds: Notts Forest, Sheffield Wednesday, Birmingham, Bolton, Doncaster and Oldham Athletic.
Wasn't Cloughie still in charge at Forest when Sheridan joined them? Yes, but Shez played just once in 4 months. Leeds should have bought him back at a snip of the £650,000 they got for him.
Why didn't they? Wilkinson was going through his non-creative period at the time. Sheridan went on to play in Europe with Wednesday and scored the winner in the 1991 Rumbelows League Cup Final.
Retired from playing: He had been appointed player/coach in 2001 by Andy Ritchie but he played his last game for Oldham aged 39 on 21 February 2004.
He deserves a medal: He actually got a demotion. Iain Dowie came in as manager and put Sheridan in charge of the youth team. When Dowie left in 2003, Sheridan managed the side for 12 games.
And? They won just twice.
Did he lose the dressing room and the respect of the players? The dressing room is still there but Brian Talbot eventually came in and made Sheridan the 1st team coach in late 2004. Other Leeds players say he was the best player they ever played with.
Hobbies: The horses.
A future Leeds manager? He has more of a chance than Peter Reid coming back for a second term.

Carl Shutt

Age: 34.
Position: Striker.
Main strengths: Good eye for goal.
Debut: At home against Bournemouth in 1989 and scored a hat trick.

Leeds must have thought they had struck gold. Where did they buy him from, Tiffany's? Bristol City but Wilkinson in his wisdom proceeded to use him in midfield.
Games: 46 (18 goals).
Era: 1988-1993.
Best remembered: That Stuggart game. Shutt's performance planted the seed for 'Loaded' magazine, apparently.
Clubs after Leeds: Birmingham, Manchester City, Bradford, and finally Darlington.
Retired: June 1999.
And never kicked a ball again? He actually went to play non-league football with Kettering in the Conference League. In 2000 as the elder statesman of the team he was given temporary charge when they went managerless.
And how did that go? Very well. He turned the team around and was given the job full-time.
How long did he last? One season.
But at least he had his foot in the door of football management? After Kettering he did some freelance scouting for various clubs until early 2004 when he got the manager's job at Bradford Park Avenue.
What league are they in? Conference North/Unibond. The job was part-time and to supplement his income he was also Commercial Manager responsible for getting advertising.
As if he hadn't got enough on his plate: He spent six hours a day on the phone doing deals.
And what if the team were short? He played. His last outing was in December 2004 when he was 43 and he even scored. He said he needed a taxi to get back to the halfway line.
Sadly: In May 2005 he was sacked when the club was relegated. They only won 5 games all season.
Family life: Carl has a son also called Carl.

Lyndon Simmonds

Age: 39.
Dream come true: Lyndon was only ever a Leeds United fan and when Eddie Gray turned up at his school in South Wales to sign him he asked where Jeremy Beadle was. He thought it was something arranged by Jim'll Fix It.

Leeds era: 1984-1987.
Debut: With two hours notice Lyndon made his debut against Portsmouth at Elland Road and scored twice.
Sensation: In those days Leeds were in Division 2 but there were no Division 1 games that day so the BBC were covering the commentary of the Leeds game live to the masses. A star was born.

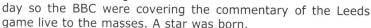

Games: 11 (3 goals).
What happened? George McCluskey came back from injury and Lyndon was packed off back to the reserves.
Other clubs: Swansea and Rochdale.
Retired: Aged just 21 in 1988.
Reason: Pelvic injury.
Gap year: Whereas some youngsters might take a year out to travel the world, Lyndon decided to have a couple of operations and lay low.
1990: It was before the mobile phone was invented and Lyndon got himself a job at a BT parts factory in South Wales. He was there for a decade and got himself to management level.
I knew of a Japanese computer chip company that was so successful they had to move to smaller premises: It was a similar case for Lyndon. BT's operation was moved to Eastern Europe and he had no choice but to take redundancy.
Did he stay out of work for long? No. He got work with a company near Newport called RF Brooks who make 18,000 meals a day for Marks & Spencer. He's there to this day as Operations Manager.
What does he do? He makes sure all those curries and shepherds pies come off the conveyor belt in tiptop condition.
Family: Lyndon's been married 10 years and has two daughters.

Ronnie Sinclair

Age: 41.
Middle name: McDonald.
Where did McDonald come from? It's a tradition clan name in the Scottish Western Isles.
Appearance: A man who still lives at home with his parents.
Position: Goalkeeper.
Era: 1986-1989.
Height: 5' 10".
A bit small for a keeper? He had springs in his feet and wore platform boots.
Games: 9. He was understudy to Mervyn Day.
A legend at: Stoke City. He was there from 1991-1996.

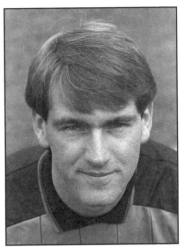

Retired: 1998 at Chester City.
Any particular reason? He sustained a knee injury and packed in aged just 31.
Keepers normally go on until they're 40: Nigel Martyn is still playing in the Premier League and he's 39.
Did Ronnie stay in the game? Yes. He always maintained good links with Stoke City and in 1998 the Stoke City manager Brian Little offered Ronnie a full-time job and he's been there ever since.
What was the job? Initially, a goalkeeping coach at the youth academy. He soon got promoted to first-team goalkeeping coach.
What does he have to do? He makes sure the first team keeper is warmed up before matches and makes sure all keepers are fit and injury free through specific training objectives.
What does he think about the current topic of blunders made by Premier League keepers? They are an inevitable part of the game. Blunders mean goals, goals mean excitement. Every time a goal goes in against Stoke he thinks it's down to him even though he is watching on the bench.
Did Ronnie make any blunders at Leeds? He didn't say he did. It was always going to be hard to get better than Merv.
Lives: Stoke.

Glynn Snodin

Age: 45.
Position: Left-back.
Style: Gritty and determined, always gave 100%.
Previous Clubs: Doncaster Rovers and Sheffield Wednesday.
Era: 1987-1992.
Appearance: Kajagoogoo fan.
Leeds high point: Turning up for work. Sounds a bit clichéd but he loved coming to the club to train even though he commuted from Doncaster.
Best perk: Nissan Bluebird. Given to him by Leeds.
Low Point: Not getting a game

when Howard Wilkinson took over. It was all Tony Dorigo's fault.
Retired: 1995 at Carlisle due to injury. Not only had the moustache and bleached hair gone but so had his legs.
Then what? Carlisle manager Mick Wadsworth gave Glynn a job as chief scout. This set Glynn on the coaching road and even today he is still taking the course to becoming a fully bona fide coaching guru with badges and certificates.
Did he progress to manager? Let's face it, at Carlisle anyone could have had a go? Michael Knighton moved in and moved Glynn out. He went over to the east coast to be youth team manager at Scarborough in 1997 and the year after went to Doncaster Rovers.
Where his brother was manager? Ian asked Glynn to be 1st team coach. No nepotism really as Glynn had the ability and the two brothers won Doncaster Rovers the Conference Cup.
The kiss of death: In 2000 the two of them were shown the door. Alan Curbishley stepped in to give Glynn a job at Premier League Charlton and he's still there as reserve team manager.
Success: Charlton's second eleven won the league title in 2005 under Glynn so he's definitely going to be one to watch in terms of management potential. Charlton is built on its youth policy so Glynn was well chuffed.
Hobbies: He likes golf, naturally, and reads a lot of sports books, mainly autobiographies.
His own book would be called? 'Snods'. Or maybe 'The Brother's Glynn'. What about 'Glynn and Tonic?'.

Ian Snodin

Age: 42.
Leeds Era: 1985-1987.
Games: 55 (Goals 8).
For the record: Ian became a club record when sold to Everton for £840,000.
Position: Midfield and right back.
Other clubs: Doncaster Rovers, Everton, Sunderland (loan), Oldham and Scarborough.
Retired: 1998 after which Ian returned to his native South Yorkshire to manage Doncaster Rovers from 1998-2000. It would have been easier being the boss of car makers MG Rover.

So it was a tough task? Snods was halfway through a two-year playing contract at Scarborough when Doncaster came knocking. Donny had just been relegated to the Conference, the chairman had been accused of burning down the stand and crowds were down to 600. Ian remembers they didn't even have a ball, nets, kit or a training ground. On August 1st he had four players to start the new season because the rest had left and the only ones still at the club couldn't find anyone to take them on!

Ben Elton could turn that into a West End farce: Ian faced an impossible task but rang around and got some old mates to play including John Sheridan, Tommy Wright, Neville Southall and Steve Nicol.

Not exactly brimming with pace: After 18 months as manager in the Conference, Ian got into radio work and was then asked by Sky to cover a Conference game at Doncaster.

A good choice: Now he is Sky's regular Conference expert as well as doing radio work covering his old club Everton.

No time for football? He's perfectly happy with his media work. His eldest son Ian, 17, has followed in the Snodin footsteps by signing for Doncaster.

Snodin on Bremner: *"Billy boosted my career without a doubt. He sold me to Leeds from Doncaster, which was a massive move for me, and then he sold me from Leeds to Everton."*

Family: Five kids. Three boys, two girls, one wife. Phew!

Gary Sprake

Age: 60.
Leeds era: 1962-1973.
Position: Goalkeeper
Games: 506.
Clean sheets: 216.
Other club: Birmingham.
Retired: 1975 aged 29.

Back from the dead: Gary is believed to be the only ex-footballer to die three times and reach the age of 60.

Death 1: On the operating table in 1975 after suffering a spinal injury playing for Birmingham at QPR. While in hospital a blood clot developed in a leg and moved to his lung where it became blocked.

Deaths 2 & 3: In 1995, he had two massive heart attacks and 'died' twice more before being revived. Two years later he underwent a quadruple heart by-pass operation.

After football: He spent nearly 25 years working for Solihull Council as a training officer, organising courses and work placements for students and the unemployed at Solihull College.

The 'Judas' tag: Gary was labelled a Judas for allegedly helping the Sunday Mirror with an investigation into Don Revie. He denies betraying Revie but is still blackballed by most of his team-mates from that era. Sprakey is disappointed he never gets involved in the Revie reunions.

Early retirement: It came in 1998 and he now lives in Solihull with his long-term partner Jackie, whom he met after his marriage to his wife Kathy ended in divorce.

Hobbies: Enjoys reading *Leeds, Leeds, Leeds* and doing charity work for the British Heart Foundation.

Careless hands: It needles him that he will always be remembered for inadvertently throwing the ball into his own net at Liverpool in front of the Kop who immediately chanted the title of Des O'Connor's hit record at the time, Careless Hands. Now he suffers from arthritis in those hands.

Sprake on Sprake: *"I can't have been that crap because I played over 500 games in the great team Don Revie built, winning nearly every medal in the game."*

Mel Sterland

Age: 43.
Appearance: Shrek.
Era: 1989-1994.
Games: 147 (20 goals)
Aka: Zico.
Party piece: The long throw-in. Also noted for his lightning runs from right back, pin-point crosses and thunderous shooting.
Other clubs: Sheffield Wednesday, Rangers and Boston United (player/manager).
Retired: 1994.
Jack of all trades: Mel was player/manager of Boston United in the Northern Premier

League for two years then became a rep for Concept Business, a Sheffield firm selling faxes, telephone systems and photo copiers and was manager of Stalybridge Celtic in the Conference. He also had a job selling industrial gases for a Bradford based company.
He's been around: Eventually with financial guru Steve Penistone, they formed a football agency called Premier Sports UK. They advise players on mortgages, pensions and transfers.
What about Mel the media man? 'Zico' used to work as a match day summariser for Radio Aire and misses the banter he had with co-presenters John Bradley and Tim White. Now he provides statistics to the Press Association, covering games at Sheff Wednesday, Chesterfield, Rotherham and Sheff United.
Happy memories: It was Wednesday supporters who first nicknamed him Zico, but when he moved to Elland Road after winning a Scottish League Championship medal with Rangers, the Leeds fans took the name on board and gave him magnificent support.
Biggest influence? Howard Wilkinson. Mel will never forget the joy of winning promotion for Leeds from the old Division 2 as champions and then winning the League Championship - all under Howard. When Mel got the job as Boston United's player/manager he immediately sought the advice of his old mentor.
Family: Mel is married to Charmaine and they live in Sheffield. They have a son, Nathan, 18, and daughter, Chantelle, 21.

Byron Stevenson

Age: 49.
Native of: Llanelli, Wales (pronounced: Lan-eff-leee).
Era: 1973-1982.
Role: Centre half, midfield, left back, right back. He had more positions than the Kama Sutra.
And why was that? None of the Leeds managers could find a suitable role for his talents. Allan Clarke eventually sent him to Birmingham in a swap for Frank Worthington and a tin of Fray Bentos.
Retired: Couldn't come quick enough in 1986 at Bristol City.
Next on the agenda: Lord

Byron returned to Leeds (he'd married a Leeds lass and she felt homesick) and went into the pub game, almost immediately taking charge of *The Angel* in Rothwell.
Time gentlemen please: After 18 months he moved to *The Golden Lion* in Pudsey and in 1989 went to *The Two Pointers* in Woodlesford. That lasted 3 years and his final boozer was *The New Inn* at Churwell. Altogether he was in the pub game until 1996.
What happened in 1996? His father was diagnosed with Parkinson's disease so Byron moved back to Llanelli.
Isn't that what Michael J Fox suffers from? It starts off with a twitching finger and gets progressively worse over a ten year period. It is also incurable. Paul Madeley has the illness too. It must be a difficult job but to his credit Byron is still caring for his father today.
What does he do for money? Byron gets a small amount as a carer but is also on the sick himself on account of a knee problem.
An old war wound probably: He still gets about though. Up until recently he was doing van deliveries for Daryl the butcher in Llanelli. He got free steaks, sausages and burgers for his services in lieu of money.
An interesting fact: Radio 1 man Chris Moyles used Byron Stevenson's name to vote for Will Young in Pop Idol.
Why didn't he use his own name? 'Coz he's in the media and he probably pretended he didn't watch it.

Dave Stewart

Age: 58.
Not to be confused with: Dave Stewart who made millions with The Eurythmics. This Dave can suck a tune but not write one.
Position: Goalkeeper.
Best known for: Keeping goal in the 1975 European Cup Final.
Era: 1973-1978.
Leeds home: Wetherby.
International caps: 1. For Scotland and he even saved a penalty.
Subsequent clubs: West Brom (under Big Ron) and Swansea (under The Tosh).

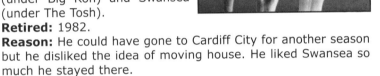

Retired: 1982.
Reason: He could have gone to Cardiff City for another season but he disliked the idea of moving house. He liked Swansea so much he stayed there.
First job: Carpet fitter for Carpet Land, Swansea.
You can't get better than a quite fit fitter? (Before he signed for Leeds he was a carpet fitter in Scotland as well as playing part-time for Ayr United). The Swansea Carpet Land job was in 1983 but the company went bust some years later.
He had the rug pulled from under him? He next got a job as a sales rep selling glasses to pubs and clubs across South Wales. That didn't last long but in 1991 he found his true vocation.
Shag piles? Goldsmith.
A 24-carat career: David was taken under the wing of a retiring old master and had 9 months to learn the trade.
Which is? Diamond setting, design, repairs, hand marking. He doesn't do watches though. The company is called Spencer Morgan and that's where he works to this day.
What about his eye sight? Well that has gone. He now wears glasses for work but he doesn't need specs for golf.
Any other signs of old age? He's in good shape. David says he's very much the same size as he was when he was at Leeds.
Maybe it's all that golf: And painting. He's a keen artist.
And does he get to watch any football? No. His boss doesn't let him have Saturdays off.

John Stiles

Age: 41.

Any relation to Nobby Stiles? That's his Dad. Johnny Giles is his uncle too so he's well connected.

It's a small world: Between the 3 of them they won every honour in the game. World Cup, European Cup, UEFA Cup, FA Cup, League Championship...

So what's John's contribution? 'Man of the Match' for Doncaster against Scarborough in 1992.

What about Leeds? He nearly won a Division 2 promotion medal but the team lost against Charlton. That was his low point at the club.

Did he possess his Father's steel and his uncle's finesse? Not quite. After 5 seasons and 81 appearances he joined Doncaster only to retire from the game in 1992 on loan at Rochdale.

I can think of better places to end it all: John then worked from 1992-1997 for Abbey Insurance in Leeds selling life insurance before becoming a football agent in 1997.

Any big names on his books? No. He used to manage one of David McNiven's boys but generally he would tout videos of up-and-coming foreign players to anyone who would entertain him. That didn't last so he took the obvious career move by becoming a stand-up comedian.

You're joking? Since 2002 he's been full-time with an agent, a website and a black tie. He was the quiet one in the Leeds dressing room too.

How much does he charge? He is working up to what Bob Monkhouse used to earn (£10,000 a night). Currently he does 4-5 nights a week and tells stories about football.

What's his best joke? He said 'he doesn't do overtime'.

Hobbies: He collects football memorabilia. In his bedroom he has Billy Bremner's shirt from the 1972 Cup Final signed by all the players.

Have you seen him in pantomime? Only when he played for Leeds United.

Gordon Strachan

Age: 48.
Appearance: The David Beckham of the bird watching world.
Position: Right-hand midfield.
Games: 244 (45 goals).
Age signed: 32.
Previous clubs: Dundee, Aberdeen and Manchester United.
Left Leeds: 1995 aged 38 for Coventry.
Retired: 1997. He was Ron Atkinson's assistant in 1995 and took charge in 1996. He was manager until 2001.
Strachan on management: *"It's like being a doctor. You are making an oath to thousands of people to make the club better."*
Did Coventry get better? Unfortunately Dr Strachan was sacked but he wasn't out of work for long and took up the reigns at Southampton.
Did he do well at The Saints? He got Southampton to an FA Cup final, eighth in the Premiership and into Europe for the first time in 19 seasons.
Terrific. Give this guy an extended contract: He didn't want one. In 2004 he quit football altogether.
To manage Bradford City? He wanted to spend more time with his family. With his wife Lesley they embarked on a tour of the world.
Like backpackers? Europe, America, Australia and together they did everything from surfing to snorkelling.
Did he miss football? Yes. As soon as he got back he applied for the Scotland job. He says he sees the game differently after a year off and on his travels he observed other athletes from other sports and how they trained, ate and lived. He said he was collecting data to prepare himself for his next management position.
Has the new position arrived? In June 2005 he took over as manager of Celtic on a 12-month rolling contract.
Football according to Gordon: *"I don't want a club striving for survival, since that requires a certain style of football. I want to play attractive football with room for playmakers."*

Frank Strandli

Age: Still only 33. He seems to have been 33 for 10 years.
Born: Norway.
Leeds era: 1993-1994. Fish & Chips were £1.29 (with scraps).
Appearance: A Norwegian Chris Moyles.
I only have eyes for Leeds: Signed from Norway's IK Staart, Frank was a member of the Norway Whites before joining the club.
Games: 16 (2 goals).
Debut: Against Middlesbrough in January 1993 and scored within eleven minutes of coming on as a sub.

What did Wilkinson see in him: On a pre-season tour in 1992, Strandli impressed when he lined-up against Leeds in Norway. Leeds did have to wait a year until Frank did his national service. Perhaps it would have been better if he'd gone missing in action. However he did play for his country 24 times.
What have Norway ever done? England haven't beaten them in any of the last five meetings.
He must have been good: He was but not at Leeds.
Other clubs: IFK Gothenburg, Lillestrom, SK Brann and Aalborg BK but where were you on Friday 22nd September 2002?
Why what happened? It was black armbands all round since it was the date Frank retired.
I can feel the tears welling up inside: Frank was forced to quit due to injury and moved back to his home of Kristiansand. On a good note his dodgy hamstring enabled him to collect over $1 million in insurance money.
Did he get fatter living off his huge payout? No, he became a big buddy of former Manchester City striker Uwe Rosler and began coaching for a club in southern Norway in 2003. He quit in spring of 2005 and now lives and coaches at his hometown club of FC Staart. The place where it all started.

Peter Swan

Age: 39.
Era: 1985-1989.
Appearances: 55 (13 goals).
Not a bad return for a defender: He was also used as an attacker on occasion.
Strengths: Heading.
Weakness: Flair.
After Leeds: Hull City, Port Vale, Plymouth, Burnley, Bury, Burnley again and York City.
Retired: 2000.
Reason: Injury.
Things to do after being a professional footballer: Well, cross off being manager of Unibond team Ossett Town. He did that but was sent on his way in 2002.

What else shall I cross off? Being a football agent. He spent 2 years working for Premier Management as an 'introducer', learning the ropes of being a football agent. He seems to have left that career on the subs bench.
What for? Procurement. He works for a Sheffield based company called Grayrose. They do interiors.
Does he mince around like that poncey Lawrence Llewellyn Bowen? Not a man like Peter Swan. He's actually the procurement manager and buys everything from toilet rolls to parquet flooring. The company do big commercial interiors like car showrooms.
How long has he been there? 12 months.
Does he still have any involvement with football? He has a coaching license and worked with Northampton's youth team in 2004 but that all changed when a new structure was set in place.
Where is he treasured? Hull. He has two regular Daily Mail features each week where he talks football. He also guest commentates for BBC Radio Humberside.
Don't let his boss at Grayrose read this bit but...: Peter is always on the lookout for a return to football. He's also considering getting involved with property development. A man on a mission. Good luck.

Bob Taylor

Age: 38.
Leeds era: 1986-1989.
Wet behind the ears: Leeds
was his first club. Other than
holidaying at Pontin's it was the
first time he had left Co. Durham
when he came to Elland Road
aged 18.
Previous jobs: Binman, Age
Concern worker. Prior to coming
to Leeds he was on the dole.
Position: Striker.
Games: 54 (13 goals).
Lived: Barwick-in-Elmet.
Other clubs: Bristol City, WBA,
Bolton and Cheltenham.
**Retired from professional
ranks:** 2003.

Did he go back on the bins? Bob had no career prospects
whatsoever when he quit professional football and waited by the
phone all the summer of 2003 for offers.
Who finally rang? Nobody. Bob got off his backside and went
to watch his local side Tamworth Town. They were managed by
a former team-mate, Mark Cooper (son of Terry) who offered
him a trial and then a part-time contract. He is still there and is
one of the Conference's leading scorers.
That's only part-time though: When he isn't training with the
team (twice a week) he is training on his own. That's what he
does. Bob goes to his local gym in Lichfield and pounds the
treadmill. He needs it to keep fit. Other than that he is taking
his coaching badge and hopes to secure a job in the summer of
2005.
Couldn't he do anything else? Bob says he couldn't. He has
no CSEs or 'O' levels but loves playing football. He even prefers
non-league to professional, saying it is less stressful and admits
he would play for nothing.
Family: Married with two children aged 14 and 9.
Hobbies: Golf and shopping.
Bob on the bins: *"In my day we had to carry those big metal
bins which weighed a ton. It's much easier now with a
wheelie bin."*
Bob on Football: *"These days if we lose I still have a pint after
the match and forget about the result."*

Gwyn Thomas

Born: Swansea.
Another Welshman: I don't know what was in the water but David Gwyn Thomas was part of a conveyor belt of Welsh talent who opted for Leeds instead of other clubs.
Age: 47.
Leeds era: 1974-1984.
Games: 104 (3 goals).
Position: Midfield.
Other clubs: Barnsley, Hull City and Carlisle.
So fruity: Gwyn has lived in Moortown, north Leeds, since 1984. He works for Direct Fruit Supplies who provide fruit and

vegetables to restaurants, hotels and delicatessens. Gwyn runs the warehouse in North Street. An acquaintance started the business and Gwyn was taken on board 12 years ago, soon after retiring from football. Now the company has 23 employees and the Thomas family table is never short of good fruit and veg!
So he didn't try to stay in the game? When he was playing part-time he intended doing a physio course but couldn't get to college and decided to pack football in.
Did he suffer from injuries at Leeds like so many others? Gwyn was rarely injured at Leeds but he damaged cruciate ligaments in both knees during his time at Barnsley. He recovered but he was never the same player after. While turning out for his works team in the gym four or five years ago his Achilles tendon snapped and it felt as if he'd been shot.
The Managers: At Elland Road, hard tackling Gwyn served under seven managers. Don Revie signed him as an apprentice but left a few weeks later to be succeeded by Brian Clough. Then came Jimmy Armfield , Jock Stein, Jimmy Adamson, Allan Clarke and Eddie Gray – all very different characters.
Any regrets? He has no regrets about playing in a different era despite the high wages taken home by today's stars. *"We took the game seriously but we also had time for a laugh and a drink and we mixed with the fans more than they do today."*
Family: Gwyn and his wife Sarah have daughters aged 22 and 16.

Mickey Thomas

Born: Mochdre, Colwyn Bay.
Age: 51.
Appearance: A young Ken Dodd.
Aka: The Welsh George Best (not for the football).
Leeds era: June 1989 to August 1990.
Games: Just 3.
Welsh caps: 51.
Other clubs: Wrexham (twice), Manchester United, Everton, Brighton, Stoke, Chelsea, West Brom, Derby, Wichita Wings (American Indoor League), Shrewsbury, Stoke, Conway United and Portmadoc(manager).

Still in front of the cameras: Before Leeds were relegated from the Premiership in 2004 he was a visitor to Elland Road in his role with Manchester United TV. That's how he operates these days as commentator, pundit and presenter. He also gets £750 a time for after-dinner speeches.

What does he talk about? Prison life. In 1993 he was jailed for 18-months for his part in a counterfeit money case in which forged notes found their way into the hands of apprentices at Wrexham FC. He served 9-months. After his arrest, spoof banknotes featuring Mickey's head, began circulating in Wales.

Mickey on counterfeiting: *"So Roy Keane's earning 50 grand a week. I was on that before police found my printing machine."* Did I mention he was also stabbed in a domestic incident?

Has his life turned into a film yet? I guess Speilberg is busy making Jaws 7. Mickey does mention that his cell mate in prison was a two-time murderer.

What about Leeds? His time there was ruined by a knee injury that struck in the third game of the club's Division 1 championship season of 1989/90. He needed a cartilage operation and later went on loan to Stoke before joining them permanently.

Memories: Scoring the winning goal for Wrexham against Arsenal in the FA Cup in January 1992, when he was 37. Another was scoring for Wales against England in a 4-1 victory.

Least likely to say: *"I'll give you change for that fifty."*

Hobbies: Sea fishing in Colwyn Bay, art and using his impish sense of humour.

Imre Viradi

Age: 46.

Leeds era: 1990-1992.

Imre Varadi sounds like a type of violin: Get your bow across this one: 'Im-re, Imre Viradi, Imre Viradi, Imre Var-a-adi Oi!'

Clubs other than Leeds: There isn't enough room to print them all. He had more clubs than Ian Woosnam. 13 in all.

Strengths: Goal scorer with pace and long hair down the back.

Car at Leeds: XR3i.

Medals: He won a Division 2 Championship medal with Leeds

but missed out the following season having not played enough games.

Retired: 1996 at Scunthorpe. He went on to manage Matlock in the Unibond League. That lasted 18 months.

Then? In 1998 he went to be Mel Sterland's assistant at Staleybridge Celtic. It was only a part-time job and it allowed him to start up his own kids' soccer school. Guess what it's called?

The 'Imre Viradi Soccer School'? Correct.

Based: In Sheffield where he also lives. He then began working for Nike and started a touring version of his soccer school. By 1999 he was going around the country showing youngsters how to develop darting runs on goal.

Never one to stand still: In 2001 Imre became a FIFA licensed agent. Today he works for Stellar Group and handles the financial affairs of some of the UK's top players including Matthew Kilgallon and Simon Walton.

Does he say "Show me the money"? Probably. Imre loves wheeling and dealing and admits he goes at it 24/7. His spare time is taken up doing the odd match commentary for Radio Aire and Radio Leeds.

Would I recognise him today? He has a Nasser Hussain hair style, he usually wears a suit.

Hobbies: Going to the gym and topping up his tan.

Married? He divorced Miss Sheffield some years back.

Ray Wallace

Born: Lewisham.
Age: 35 (born five minutes after twin brother Rod).
Leeds era: 1991-1994.
Games: 7.
Role: To provide company for his more successful brother who signed who Leeds signed as a 2-for-1 package from Southampton in 1991. Rod costing £1.6 million, Ray costing £100,000.

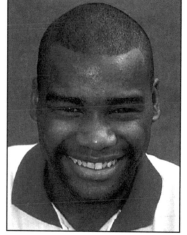

Did it work? Rod was a great success at Leeds so you have to say it did, but Ray must have hoped to play more games than he did.

Other clubs: Southampton, Swansea (loan), Reading (loan), Stoke and Hull City (loan).
Position: Right back.
Retired: 1999.
No resentment: Although Ray won four England Under-21 caps at Southampton, his career never rose to the heights of his brothers Rod and Danny. There was never any resentment and the trio remained very close.
Fit and not so fit: Ray and Rod have greatly supported former Southampton, Manchester United and England star Danny who suffers from multiple sclerosis and walks with the aid of a stick. By an ironic contrast, Ray is a fitness trainer at a health centre in the Greater Manchester area.
Coaching: Ray has qualified as a UEFA 'B' category coach and was working with the youth team at Bolton for 18-months. That didn't last but he hopes he will be able to return to football.
Career highlight: *"Playing with two of my brothers in the Southampton 1st team for the first time."*
A legend: If that can be said about Ray then it would have been at Stoke where he saw out his career playing 179 times for the club. He later played non-league football in and around Manchester for Tyldesley.
Favourite Leeds player: David Batty.
Superstitions: Ray was always the last player out of the tunnel and ate chicken and beans as pre-match meal.

Rod Wallace

Born: Lewisham.
Aka: Hot Rod.
Age: 35.
Leeds era: 1991-1998.
Games: 255 (66 goals).
Striking partner: Lee Chapman.
Role: With blistering pace he would run round defenders, latch on to errors and chase down flick-ons. Sometimes he would even take the ball with him.
Other clubs: Southampton, Rangers, Bolton and Gillingham.
He must have scored plenty at Gillingham given his pedigree? Rod's time there

was punctuated by injury and in two seasons he only played 27 times. He scored 12 goals though.
Retired: 2004 due to injury.
And then what? House renovating in Epsom but Rodney is open to offers. He would love a job back in football especially as soccer runs in the family. Elder brother Danny played for Southampton and Manchester United and twin brother Ray joined Leeds from the Saints, although Rod cost a tribunal fixed £1.6million, while Ray was valued at £100,000. Rod is also taking his coaching qualifications.
Record breaker: The three brothers once made history by playing in the same match for Southampton's first team.
Boot boy: As an apprentice at Southampton, one of Rod's jobs was to clean the boots of former Leeds striker Joe Jordan. It was a menial task but Joe was such a good tipper.
Pick of the bunch: His Goal of the Season against Spurs at Elland Road in 1994. He beat several opponents before scoring with a deadly accurate shot.
So does he play any football these days? *"I picked up a few injuries at Gillingham so I don't want to risk doing any further damage. Besides, I saw some of the old Leeds players in the Six-a-Side Masters recently and there were a lot of bodies around that were, how shall I put it, on the big side!"*
Rod keeps fit: By working out in the gym and he and wife Rachel are kept busy looking after their three children McKenzie, aged 3, Macey, 5, and Morgan, 8.

Andy Watson

Age: 46.
Born: Aberdeen.
Leeds era: 1983-1985. The Division 2 days.
Reason for inclusion: Eddie Gray wanted some midfield class and Watson arrived at the club with a UEFA Cup winners medal around his neck.
Verdict: Not great.
Reason: Poor first touch but he did give 100%.
Games: 43 (7 goals).
Other clubs: Aberdeen, Hearts and Hibernian.
All Scottish clubs: He never really settled south of the border. Leeds wasn't big on fried mars bars so he was happy to move back to Scotland at the earliest opportunity. He did say he really enjoyed his time at Leeds.
Retired: 1989 due to knee trouble aged just 28.
What's he doing now? Assistant Manager at Rangers to Alex McLeish (aka Horatio in CSI:Miami). The two joined The Dons on the same day in 1976 and when McLeish took over as Hibs' manager in 1998, he made his old team mate his assistant.
And how has it been going? Great. Andy was just getting over celebrating Rangers' title win the week before.
What's their management style like? Who plays the good cop? *"We're both thoroughly good guys."*
Any 'hairdryer' rants in the style of their former manager at Aberdeen Alex Ferguson? *"He may be the reason I have no hair today. I am as bald as a coot."*
What about the moustache though? *"I left that at Leeds."*
A proud achievement: Andy's hasn't worked outside the game now for 30 years. Maybe he should have a testimonial. He doesn't get too much time for anything other than football and he was speaking to us from Germany where he was attending the opening of Bayern Munich's new stadium which is said to be the best in the world.
It's a small world: Andy played alongside Gordon Strachan at Aberdeen (not Leeds) and the two will be on opposing sides when they meet at next season's Old Firm games.

David White

Age: 38.
Leeds era: 1993-1995.
Appearance: YTS trained male stripper.
Position: Right wing/midfield.
Where seen: Treatment table.
Games: 51 (11 goals).
Bought by: Howard Wilkinson.
Role: Supply chain for Brian Deane and Rod Wallace.
Manager would say: *"He'll show his Man City form in the next game."*
Blinkered: Leeds fans never really saw the best of his attacking ability.
Another bad purchase? When David signed for Leeds he actually warned the club that there were problems with his right ankle.
They didn't heed his advice?: Two operations later and his Leeds career never really got out of the blocks. A fracture to his left heel hardly helped matters. He's the only player to have a twin town.
Which one? Holby City.
After Leeds? Sold to Sheffield United in 1995. His last game was the 1997 play-off final.
Retired: 1998.
Were his ankles shot to pieces by that time? Poor David has chronic arthritis in them. Fortunately, he's from an astute family with a solid business background so David's become part of that now his playing days are over.
What do they do? Many fingers in many pies. As well as the company called 'Uniquety' which deals in events/corporate hospitality there is also a very successful trade in dealing in Manchester's waste and scrap.
Plenty of that in Manchester: They're called White Reclamation. 'Uniquety' do functions and also hire out fancy villas in Spain. David is the front man of the more sporting side of the operation.
Any lingering footballing ties? As is standard these days he does corporate match day work and the occasional co-commentating on local radio. All Manchester City based where he is still considered a hero.

Chris Whyte

Age: 43.
Leeds era: 1990-1993.
Nickname: Huggy Bear.
Not related: To sponsors Whyte & Mackay although I bet he wishes he was.
Medals: Division 1 Championship medal 1991/92.
Games: 146 (6 goals).
Position: Central defence.
Other clubs: Arsenal, Los Angeles Lazers, West Brom, Birmingham, Charlton, Detroit Neon, Leyton Orient, Oxford United and Rushden & Diamonds.
Retired: 2001.

What did he do in the US? Chris had a couple of spells playing indoor football in America at Los Angeles and Detroit.

Did his clearances hit the roof? Chris did okay and loved the life but missed playing the real thing back in England so home he came.

Retirement: 1999.

Home: Whytey now lives in Enfield.

Works: As a chauffeur driving busy executives around the capital. He works for a husband and wife team and that's the job he's been doing since ending his footballing career at Rushden & Diamonds at the age of 37.

Ambition: He hankers after a return to the game having gained his coaching badge. The problem is that his hours as a chauffeur make it difficult to get regular time off.

He'd look good driving to the training ground in his Rolls Royce: He doesn't drive a Rolls Royce and he isn't allowed to drive his employer's vehicle except on chauffeuring business.

That own goal: Chris was a big favourite with Leeds fans when he was at Elland Road and he became even more popular when, while playing for Birmingham, he gifted the Whites an own-goal winner in the first leg of the 1996 Coca Cola Cup semi-final, at St Andrews. United went on to win the tie 5-1 on aggregate.

Chris on Leeds: *"I have to pinch myself to believe what has happened to Leeds United over the last few years. They've been through a dreadful time since competing in the Champions League but they're a big club and they'll come back again."*

David Whyte

Age: 46.
Aka: Who?
I don't remember him: He played just twice before he fell out of favour with Jimmy Armfield then Jock Stein then Jimmy Adamson.
Era: 180 minutes some time between 1977-1979.
Position: Midfield.
Debut: Against Aston Villa.
The boy never stood a chance: There were some outstanding players at the club even then and only the best was good enough.
Other clubs: Hibernian, Bradford City and Barnsley.
Retired: 1982.
Part-timer: David played on at Northwich and the money received as a semi-professional was enough to tide him over.
Until when? 1983 when he joined the fire service. David was a rare breed of ex-Leeds pros actually playing Sunday morning football on Beeston Rec. One of his team mates was also a fireman and that's how his interest in the fire service began.
Where was he based? Initially he went to Castleford from 1983-1988. His first fire was a mattress on the side of the road. Today it would have been a car.
Where did he go after Castleford? Moortown which is where he is stationed today. He only has 7 years to go before he can retire although he is still a fireman he does get to drive the engine once in a while and you have to be fit to do the job.
Did he ever get called down to Elland Road when the O'Leary babes were 'on fire'? It was O'Leary himself who put out those flames.
What are his shifts? Are you really interested?
No. Does he keep in contact with any other Leeds players? None that we would know but he sees Neil Parker who now runs a newsagents in Leeds.
Hobbies: Golf. He plays as a member at Scarcroft GC. They are the first golf club in the UK to have a total ban on smoking.
Lives: Bardsey, Leeds, and his local is the Duke of Wellington in East Keswick.

Andy Williams

Born: Birmingham.
Age: 43.
Leeds era: 1988-1992.
Games: 61 (5 goals).
Position: Midfield.
Other clubs: Take a deep breath. Dudley Town, Solihull Borough, Coventry, Rotherham (twice), Port Vale, Notts County, Huddersfield Town, Hull City, Scarborough, Gainsborough, Matlock Town, Guiseley. Andy is available for weddings, funerals and barmitzvahs.
Retired: 1997.
Don't ask him to sing: Unlike his namesake, Andy's no

crooner, though everyone who hears his name asks him to sing a few notes. His answer is always the same: *"If I had his money I wouldn't be working for Rotherham Council!"*. Andy's job involves managing rent arrears, advising tenants and training staff. He avoided going into coaching or managing when he finished playing as he was never a good watcher.

Exam at Elland Road: After his first stint with Rotherham Council he left to become a financial advisor and passed his exam at Elland Road. Then he returned to Rotherham Council where he worked his way up to his present position.

Injury free? He never broke a bone during his professional career but was helping out a Sunday team just before Christmas, 2004, when he broke an ankle.

Top manager: Andy left United during their Championship season of 1991-92 because with Gordon Strachan, Gary McAllister, Gary Speed and David Batty around there was no prospect of regular first team football, although there is no bitterness and he rates Howard Wilkinson the best manager he has played for. Howard was especially good at getting the right people around him and signing Gordon Strachan was a masterstroke, says Andy who played his part in the promotion team in 1989-90.

Hobbies: Andy enjoys playing golf but is struggling to get his handicap below 18. *"The lower handicappers make it look so effortless but it takes a lot of practice and patience."*

Gary Williams

Age: 45.

Leeds era: 1987-1990.

Games: 45 (3 goals).

Position: Right back.

Leeds jinx: Here was another player plagued by injury during his time at the club. When he left Elland Road he remained injury free.

A quality acquisition: Gary is the proud owner of a European Cup winners medal and a League Championship medal from his time at Aston Villa, where he spent most of his career before joining Leeds. The medals are in a bank vault so he very rarely sees them.

Other clubs: The Villa, Walsall (loan), Watford, Bradford City and Golden (Hong Kong).

Hong Kong? Gary played for a team called Golden, along with Mike Duxbury. He stayed there for a year.

Retired: 1995. Before returning to England he lived in Spain for two years, coaching in international schools and playing part-time for Fuengirola, near Marbella.

Big softie: Gary has long had an interest in IT software so when he returned to England his former Villa and Leeds colleague Brendan Ormsby, who was working for Emis at the time, helped him get a job with them. Emis are the biggest suppliers of medical software in the UK. Gary has worked for them for seven years and is employed at their head office at Fulford Grange, Rawdon.

Reunions: Gary returns to Villa for anniversaries of the European Cup and League Championship successes.

Family: Gary, his wife Liz and children Simon, 21, Daniel, 18, and Natasha, 14, still live at Scarcroft where he settled when he signed for Leeds. He rented out the house when he went to Watford and abroad. Simon played in midfield for a team in Finland called Kokta for 18 months but it didn't work out and he is back home.

Head of hair: Gary is still the proud owner of a mop of curly black hair, even at 44 years of age, so Leeds fans would easily recognise him.

Frank Worthington

Age: 57.
Leeds era: 1982.
Appearance: Roadie for a Thin Lizzy covers band.
Games: 35 (Goals: 15).
Footballing legend: Scored what many say was the best goal ever. Bolton against Ipswich in 1979.
England caps: 8.
Arrived at Leeds: In a swap deal, with Byron Stevenson going to Birmingham.
Other clubs: Huddersfield, Leicester, Bolton, Birmingham, Sunderland, Southampton, Brighton,Tranmere (player/manager), Preston and Stockport.

Non-league and overseas clubs: Capetown Spurs, Tampa Bay Rowdies, Chorley, Stalybridge Celtic, Galway United, Weymouth, Radcliffe Borough, Guiseley, Preston (coach), Hinckley Town (player/coach), Cemaes Bay, Halifax Town (player/coach), Swindon (coach).
Retired (English football league): 1988.
Retired (the high life): Not just yet.
Have boots will travel: Flamboyant Frank is currently entertaining football fans and businessmen all over the world with colourful tales of his life on-and-off the pitch. His after-dinners have taken him to unusual venues such as Dubai, the Caribbean, and oil rigs off the Scottish coast.
His book: 'One Hump Or Two' was a Number One best seller in the UK. In it, Frank made no secret of his womanising and laddish lifestyle.
Any regrets? Frank has lived life to the full and it's been a real roller coaster ride. He's had his down times - being declared bankrupt in 1994 and sacked as player/manager of Tranmere by the club's administrator despite doing a good job. But the good times have outweighed the bad.
Page Three: Married to former Page Three model Carol Dwyer.
Lives: Near Huddersfield.
Elvis fan: There is no bigger admirer of the late, great Elvis Presley than Frank who has a large collection of Elvis memorabilia. To Frank, Elvis will always be 'The King'.

Nigel Worthington

Age: 43.
Born: Northern Ireland.
Position: Left-back.
Era: 1994-1996.
Arrived at Leeds: Aged 33.
Aka: The lager top of football management.
Dictionary definition of a 'Nigel': Quiet, unassuming, safe.
Role: To deputise for an ever absent Tony Dorigo.
Other clubs: Notts County, Sheffield Wednesday, Stoke and Blackpool.
Retired: 1997.
First job: At Blackpool as

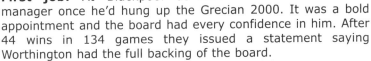

manager once he'd hung up the Grecian 2000. It was a bold appointment and the board had every confidence in him. After 44 wins in 134 games they issued a statement saying Worthington had the full backing of the board.

He was sacked? It was a mutual parting of the ways.

To where? Norwich City as number 2 to Bryan Hamilton in 2000 who himself got the boot shortly after Nigel's arrival.

Did that leave Norwich in a mess? He was installed as caretaker-boss of Norwich and on New Year's Day 2001 Worthington was given the job full-time. They were languishing in 15th place of the old Division 2. Things started to pick up however and in 2004 he got them into the Premier League.

Well done. I bet he went and bought some players for silly money: Apart from a bid for Craig Bellamy, Worthington's backers were saving themselves for the drop which occurred in May 2005.

Let's be 'avin' you: Delia Smith is a majority shareholder there but she's publicly stated Nigel Worthington will keep his job despite the relegation. He did well to get them there as a cheap and unfashionable club.

What's his secret? He mixes youthful exuberance with experience.

Why doesn't he sign Brian Deane? They already have someone to pick up the balls after training.

Hates: The sunshine and sunburn is a constant danger. He has to apply factor 50 just to stand under a light bulb.

Tommy Wright

Age: 39 and getting younger by the day.
Seasons at Leeds: 4.
Debut: 1982 against Fulham. He was only told an hour before the game he was playing.
Did his shirt fit? Like a glove.
Style: Nippy winger with an eye for a goal.
How many? 28 in 92 games.
Appearance: Blue Peter presenter. Still looks 16.
Low point: Being diagnosed as having a pelvic injury when in fact he had a rib injury. It was in the days before scans.

Other clubs: Oldham, Leicester, Middlesbrough, Bradford and Doncaster.
Retired: 1999 at Doncaster.
Then what? His good friend John Sheridan called him up and offered him the job as youth coach at Oldham, and he's still there today.
It's who you know not what you know: Tommy knew his stuff though and part of his job is to tell some of the under-16 wannabees they won't make the grade.
Do they cry? Tommy cries with them.
Sounds a bit like Pop Idol. How many get offered apprenticeships? Of the 16 lads he coaches at under-16 level each year only 6 get offered a contract.
Biggest regret: Not having anything to fall back on career wise himself. All his eggs are in the football and coaching basket.
Does he do anything else apart from coach young kids? Oldham also send him off on scouting missions to watch young players. He then writes up a report of their performance and gives it to the boss.
Mistaken ID: Tommy gets mail from another Tommy Wright (the former Man City goalkeeper). Letters from America asking him about his ancestors are forwarded to the Irish keeper and vice versa.
Married: Yes, with 3 kids - they live in Wakefield. His wife used to be one of the Hill's Angels. You remember Benny Hill?
Does Tommy chase her around the park? No, he leaves all his exercise for the gym and the football pitch.

Tony Yeboah

Age: 39
Languages: French, German and English.
German? He played for Eintract Frankfurt for 4 years before joining Leeds - his only English club.
Leeds Era: 1995-1997.
Impact: Immense. He scored some fantastic goals.
Weakness: A bit lazy.
Claim to fame: He scored Leeds' greatest ever goal as voted by the supporters. 21st August 1995 is the day we all remember where we were.
Like the day Kennedy was shot? Yeboah actually flew in to Leeds from his home in Ghana to collect the award.

What happened when he left Leeds? He went back to Germany and then a quickstep into semi-retirement in Qatar.
For what reason? He was found guilty of not paying any taxes by a German court and fined £114,000.
Retired: 2002. He went back home to his mansion in East Legon, near Accra.
To run a pub? Hardly. Yeboah has God like status in Ghana and helped run soccer schools via a company called Sportventurer.
That's nice of him: In 2003 he opened his own hotel called 'Yegoala' in Accra.
Does it have Leeds United themed rooms? The George Graham has two entrances so you can make a quick exit out of the back door. The Harry Kewell room has water which runs hot and then cold for a long time. The Seth Johnson Suite is £5,000 a night. Each Leeds room has a goldfish.
Really? No but prices do vary. Rooms start at £50.
So things are rosey? So-so. He was conned out of £100,000 in 2003 when he bought some land that the seller never actually owned. We live and learn.
But he can't be short of money: He's a celebrity. Even estate agents sell houses saying *"not far from Tony Yeboah's estate"*. He also has a property development company and a hospitality business in the city.
Family: Wife Tasha and 4 children.

Terry Yorath

Age: 55.
Full name: Terence Charles Yorath.
Position: Left-midfield.
Appearances: 197 (12 goals)
International caps: 59.
Strengths: Tackling, work rate.
Weaknesses: Pace, vision, attacking (the goals not players).
Leeds era: 1967-1976.
After Leeds: Coventry, Spurs, Vancouver Whitecaps, Bradford.
Swapping beautiful Vancouver for Bradford – was he extradited? No, Bradford's chairman, Bob

Martin, invited him to team-up with manager Trevor Cherry as player/coach, and he jumped at the chance.
Retired from playing: 1984.
Was he a good coach? The Cherry/Yorath combo did well at Bradford gaining promotion in 1985 - the year of the Valley Parade fire.
Then? Wanting to try his hand at being the 'main man' he was taken on as Swansea City manager in 1986.
No tougher job in football: 2 years later the team won promotion to Division 3. In 1988 Terry became manager of Wales.
The ultimate in Welsh football: Brian Clough said 'No', Yorath said 'Yes'. He was in charge from 1988-1993.
So he was managing two clubs? On and off. Just because he was the 'King of Wales' it didn't exclude him from being sacked at Swansea which was the case in 1991.
Other managerial ports of call? Bradford (again), Cardiff, Malaya, Japan, Lebanon, Huddersfield, Bradford and Sheff Wed. Sometimes manager, sometimes assistant to the manager.
And today? He's back at Huddersfield as assistant manager.
Books: In 2004 Terry co-wrote *Hard Man, Hard Knocks.* He's had some tragedy in his life and Terry said the book was like "*self-counselling*". The newspapers say he's 'jinxed'.
Where can we see Terry today? Doing his community service for a drink/driving offence at Middleton Park Equestrian Centre.
Where we won't see Terry? Behind the steering wheel.

The Final Whistle

So there you have it. Over 140 former players and enough careers advice to make the Employment Secretary jealous. You have to admit, all the guys are heroes.

By way of a repayment for all the great memories they have given us, some enterprising young fan should organise a Remembrance Day service for all former players. One day a year (first Sunday after March 4th) where we could gather together to pay our respects to those who had gotten muddy in battle for the sake of this great club. Instead of poppies we would pin blue sock tags to our lapels. The Very Reverend Archbishop of East Hunslet could lead us in song as we embrace the hymn 'Marching On Together'. At three o'clock there would be a seven-minute silence as we remember each goal that went in against Southampton in 1972.

Then there would be a march. London has Whitehall, Leeds has Whitehall Road. Up past the Billy Bremner statue and in to Peter Lorimer's place for a drink. Norman Hunter could do the commentary alongside David Dimbleby and the whole occasion would be live on Sky and Radio Aire.

When that went off-air we all could carry on. Wayne Entwhistle could provide the pork pies. Dylan Kerr could DJ with John Stiles providing some smiles on stage (accompanied by Kevin Hird on guitar). Tony Yeboah would fly in to sort out the hotel accommodation and George McCluskey could taxi everyone home in the morning.

If only Bob Geldof and Midge Ure were Leeds United fans.